A Toolbox *for Our*
DAUGHTERS

A Toolbox *for Our* DAUGHTERS

Building Strength, Confidence, and Integrity

Annette Geffert
and Diane Brown

NEW WORLD LIBRARY
NOVATO, CALIFORNIA

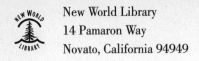

New World Library
14 Pamaron Way
Novato, California 94949

Copyright © 2000 by Annette Geffert and Diane Brown
Front cover and interior design by Mary Ann Casler
Typography by Tona Pearce Myers
Edited by Gina Misiroglu

Library of Congress Cataloging-in-Publication Data
Geffert, Annette, 1960–
  A toolbox for our daughters : building strength, confidence, and integrity / by Annette Geffert and Diane Brown.
    p. cm.
Includes bibliographical references and index.
ISBN 1-57731-120-5 (alk. Paper)
1. Daughters. 2. Girls—Conduct of life. 3. Child rearing. 4. Parent and child.
I. Brown, Diane, 1951–

HQ777 G44 2000
649'.133—dc   00-055898

First Printing, October 2000
ISBN 1-57731-120-5
Printed in Canada on acid-free paper
Distributed to the trade by Publishers Group West

10   9   8   7   6   5   4   3   2   1

*We dedicate this book to
all who strive to make better decisions
and live a life of honor and integrity.*

Contents

Acknowledgments

We want to acknowledge an incredible team of people who helped us turn our vision into a reality.

First, thanks to our publisher, New World Library, for giving two new authors a wonderful opportunity, and to our editor, Gina Misiroglu, for her insight and guidance. Thanks to the great team of people who helped put the book together: Georgia Hughes, Mary Ann Casler, Tona Pearce Myers, and Barbara King, the book's copy editor. Also, with deep appreciation and love, we thank our families for their continued love and support. We could not have written this without them.

Finally, a special thanks to the young women and their families who generously shared their stories. They are an inspiration to us. To honor their confidentiality, the names and details have been changed.

Introduction

"**I**f you want to stir up a hornet's nest, just ask mothers, 'Who are harder to raise — boys or girls?' The answer will depend on whether they're raising boys or girls. I've had both, so I'll settle the argument once and for all. It's girls.... Girls can slam a door louder, beg longer, turn tears on and off like a faucet, and invented the term, 'You don't trust me.'" Whether or not you agree with this humorous morsel of wisdom from Erma Bombeck, the general message is clear: Raising daughters is difficult.

When we first thought about writing *A Toolbox for Our Daughters,* our intention was to explore the issue of why our daughters suffer more than boys from low self-esteem and why it plummets during early adolescence. We were astounded at the overwhelming evidence of declining self-esteem, not only in the research but in what we personally observed. We began to notice this crisis in the daughters of our friends, our associates, and our own families. The problem seemed rampant and ubiquitous. It transcended all socioeconomic differences. Not only were our daughters losing their self-worth, but our society was losing in direct proportion to the quantity of girls lost in this crisis.

In examining our findings, we were surprised when a universal theme emerged repeatedly: The more poor choices young women made, the lower their self-esteem. The lower their self-esteem, the more poor choices they made. Does making poor choices cause poor self-image? Or does having a poor self-image cause poor choices? Who knows? What matters is that the results are the same — a downward spiral. Conversely, we observed that good decisions feed self-worth and lend a sense of assurance that whatever comes along can be handled. As the confidence level increases, not only are decisions handled more competently, but the consequences of making a mistake do not have such a negative impact on our daughters' self-worth. From this, we concluded that we must teach our daughters the art of making competent decisions. By doing this, we could dramatically improve the course of our daughters' lives, as well as the society in which we live.

We teach our daughters how to tie their shoes, brush their teeth, and clean their rooms. We give them instruction on how to ride a bike, how to swim, and how to drive a car. We try to give them concrete skills they will need to make their lives better. However, we often fail to teach them how to deal with life's problems effectively. We often sit back and expect them to make competent decisions in a complicated world without any real instruction.

As parents, we cannot depend on society to teach and nurture our daughters. And as parents, we cannot expect society to save them. Society is an integral part of the problem. There is an old African saying, "It takes a village to raise a child." But what type of child would "the village" raise if the village were filled with toxicity? It is this very "village" that is crippling our daughters. Can we entrust our most precious gifts to this culture?

If you answered this question with an emphatic no, then *A Toolbox for Our Daughters* is written for you. This book shows you how to move with love and authority in your daughter's life and teach her personal responsibility. It empowers you to make a difference in her life and improve your relationship with her.

But more than a practical guide for your parental relationship, this book is about giving your daughter power. Properly equipped, your daughter's success will not depend on her ability to conform to society's unrealistic expectations. She can build a life of purpose and value through her personal vision, her inner guide, and her belief in herself. If you teach your daughter how to use her decision-making tools, she can avoid victimization and the victim mentality, learn how to handle adversity, and build her character. Your daughter will learn how to survive in this world one way or another, either from society or from you. If you can teach your child how to make good decisions (ones that strengthen her character), you will teach her how to survive.

So, you may be saying, "This all sounds great in theory, but how can we actually teach our daughters to make good decisions?" We found that the best way to help our daughters escape the downward spiral of self-esteem is to provide them with specific decision-making skills and life tools — skills and tools that enhance self-esteem and lend a sense of empowerment. And we chose skills easy enough to use today and extraordinary enough to use throughout life. These strategies are tried-and-true methods tested in home workshops by parents who, like us, struggle to raise strong, confident daughters in a complex world.

The principles found behind these strategies are not new. They are simple truths that are probably familiar to you. You see them in action daily and use them regularly. What we have done is give you a framework — a place to start, inspiration to motivate you, and a plan of action that you can customize to fit your unique situation with your daughter. While we don't pretend to know all the answers, we have converted the principles we have observed into practical strategies that can help you assess where you and your daughter are, where you want to go, and how you can get there.

To describe these strategies and life skills fully, we employ a tool analogy in this book. Because tools make jobs more efficient and build stronger, more precise structures, the tool concept works well in explaining how our daughters can build strong, self-sufficient lives. But we realized that most women do not have their own tools. We both recalled instances where we stood on the couch hammering a nail into the wall with the heel of our shoe. We accomplished the task, the picture was hung, but it would have been much easier and more efficient with a hammer and a step ladder. Although we, as women, may creatively improvise tools that we lack, we benefit greatly by having the correct tools of our own.

Having and knowing how to use the proper tools is not just for hanging pictures more efficiently. Just as we need tools to build strong buildings, our daughters need tools to build strong lives. The tool analogy helps to make these tools and life skills more concrete. We anticipate that the parallelism between real tools and the life skills in this book will help you visualize these strategies as real working instruments that your daughter can pick up and use.

These tools function with your daughter's inner guide to build a foundation of strength and reliability. Each tool works best when fueled by a sense of pragmatic optimism — a knowledge that whatever comes along can be handled. Learning these skills teaches your daughter to improve the way she reacts to situations and prompts her to take personal responsibility.

A Toolbox for Our Daughters tackles the tough job of parenting girls by showing you how to

1. Create a family environment that includes security, unconditional love, and realistic boundaries where your daughter can develop a healthy self-image
2. Help your daughter learn how to make good decisions by developing her own inner support system called the Connected Inner Guide
3. Use down-to-earth power tools and convey step-by-step formulas to help your daughter face the challenges of everyday life.

This book's hands-on approach is designed for your practical use. Every chapter includes realistic, easy-to-implement strategies that really work. Supplementing these are words of wisdom and comments from professionals, parents, and teens. Included are stories to inspire you and sidebars you can review at a glance. Boxed suggestions called "Tips from the Toolbox" are added to motivate and call you to action.

A Toolbox for Our Daughters is written to parents, for parents, and in some cases with parents. The exercises at the end of each chapter called "Honing the Skills" are customized for you to do with your preadolescents and older teens. The interactive nature of these exercises provides you and your daughter with practical applications of the principles found within each chapter. The multidimensional, personal approach allows you to sit down and read in depth or simply pick up a few tips on the run. This book was designed with your hectic schedule in mind, giving you efficient, common-sense ways to help your daughter.

These practical concepts can be applied no matter what stage or state your daughter is in. Preadolescence is the ideal time to help your daughter learn the decision-making skills and life tools found within *A Toolbox for Our Daughters*. However, it is never too late to help your daughter.

You may just be looking for a few suggestions to enhance your relationship with your daughter or you may feel you have lost your daughter completely. Even if you are dealing with serious issues, these suggestions can breathe hope into your situation and help you overcome a multitude of problems.

This book is just one of many resources available to you. To be an effective parent, you will want to use a combination of resources including other articles and books, discussions with parents, conversations with your daughter, and a professional support system when appropriate. However, for most of life's trials and tribulations, the strategies found in this book can smooth out many of the rough spots.

Using this book together, you and your daughter can build a foundation of strength and promise, confidence and integrity. This does not happen overnight. So, let's get started.

Chapter One

PARENTING NUTS AND BOLTS
Building Security with Love and Boundaries

"Parents can only give good advice or put them on the right paths, but the final forming of a person's character lies in their own hands." — Anne Frank

"My mom is constantly nagging me for the details of my life, but she can't handle the truth," complains Hannah, a bright-eyed, intuitive twelve-year-old. Hannah is sure her mother cannot possibly understand the obstacles she faces every day. "If I told her half of what went on in the real world, she wouldn't let me out of the house! My day starts with me running around trying to find something to wear. I hate all my clothes. Nothing fits right. Then, my mom gripes about me being late. I hate to miss the bus because then I have to listen to her complain even longer. It's not my fault. My house is pure chaos in the morning. Then, when I get to school, my locker won't lock, so I have to carry my books around all day so that nobody steals them. And during English the other day, the cops came and arrested Eric for carrying a gun to school. Mom just has no idea. By the time I get home from school, I'm exhausted. And just when I start to relax, Mom grills me about my day. There are some things I would like to tell her if she could handle it, but she can't. She just doesn't understand. My mom thinks she knows how it is for me, but she is clueless."

Hannah's words, "You just don't understand!" are probably the most echoed phrase of adolescents. These ageless words sum up the frustration of teenagers and their parents who would like to talk to each other but can't. A 1996 *USA Today* survey indicates that 76 percent of families polled find little or no communication between parents and their teenagers. Hannah is a typical girl facing the challenges of being a teen today. Her world is complicated and confusing not only to Hannah, but also to an entire generation of girls and their parents.

Hannah's mother, Karen, like many mothers across the nation, worries about her changing relationship with her daughter. She knows there is a problem, but she is not sure how to solve it. In her words, "At times, I am afraid I'm losing my daughter. Hannah and I used to be so close, but things have really changed between us. It seems the harder I try, the worse things get. I've read every self-help book, watched all the talk shows, and tried everything I can think of, but I just can't reach her. I don't understand what's happening. She used to talk nonstop about her day. But now, when I ask her anything, I'm lucky to get a response at all. I know things aren't easy for kids her age, but they never have been. I remember the ups and downs of being young and I know I could help her if she'd just talk to me."

Karen does not understand and Hannah won't talk to her. Both are painfully aware of their deteriorating relationship. Neither knows what to do about it.

Like Karen, you may be wondering what is going on with your adolescent daughter. Just when you think you have it figured out, your daughter throws you a curve ball. You may have thought you were playing soccer only to find yourself standing at home plate holding a bat. Welcome to the confusing world of parenting an adolescent, where the games and the rules change like the weather.

Young girls and mothers across the nation are confronting similar challenges. Know that you are not alone. Parenting is rarely an easy task. Many times, the parent-adolescent relationship is a battle of wills, fraught with crises and dilemmas, even when you both have the best intentions. Parents can easily make mistakes in this unpredictable environment. Often, your daughter considers you the enemy during a time she may need you the most. And, you fear the situation and push too hard. It is no wonder your daughter's self-esteem and your patience can plummet during this tumultuous time.

Are the problems your daughter faces the same ones you faced as a teen? The answer is both yes and no. Life is not as simple as it used to be. The challenges and worries that you faced as a teen take on new meaning with the complexities of today's world. Girls still worry about the same things they always did — physical appearance, popularity, boyfriends, grades, friendships. But now they might also contend with children wielding guns, abusive boyfriends, sexually transmitted diseases, substance abuse, and eating disorders. Where previous generations valued women and children and protected them from harm, modern society devalues and victimizes women in unprecedented numbers. Today's world is not a very friendly place for teens, especially girls.

Society cultivates an environment for our daughters where extremes can become the norm. Dieting becomes bulimia. Depression becomes suicide. And sexual activity can lead to death.

Thanks to society's narrow and unrealistic expectations, many of our daughters have an equally unrealistic and unhealthy view of their bodies. Society's picture of the ideal woman is getting thinner and thinner. In fact, many teenage girls' primary focus is to lose weight. Society's prescribed image of a size 4 model fuels this desire. This image is incongruent with the fact that today the majority of American women wear a size 12 or larger. Striving to achieve an unrealistic body weight, coupled with the onset of puberty, can twist dieting into excessive behaviors such as anorexia and bulimia. Some researchers estimate that the incidence of eating disorders increased by 50 percent in the 1990s. The vast majority, more than 90 percent, of the those in the United States with eating disorders are young women and teenage girls.

More than one-quarter of all young women feel depressed regularly, and approximately four out of one hundred teenagers get seriously depressed each year. In a study by *USA Today,* 28 percent of surveyed young women ages fifteen to twenty-one feel depressed either daily or a few times a week. The acting out of depression can range from low self-esteem and difficulty in school, to violence and substance abuse, to the extreme of suicidal thoughts and attempts. It is not uncommon for depression to lead to tragic conse-quences.

Sexual activity among adolescents has always been a concern for parents as well as society. However, with more teens sexually active and the presence of deadly sexually transmitted diseases (STDs), the stakes are much higher.

> ## THOUGHT FOR PARENTS TO LIVE BY
>
> Everything you do teaches your daughter the philosophy of how to live.

According to a study by the Alan Guttmacher Institute, a leading source for research data on reproductive health issues, 80 percent of adolescents begin having intercourse, with the likelihood increasing steadily with age. Of these sexually experienced teens, about one in four acquires an STD. Tragically, many sexually transmitted diseases are incurable and some, such as AIDS, are deadly. The world has changed, the risks are higher, and our daughters are at stake.

Within this complex society, our daughters are trying to grow up. As they develop their unique identity and form their value systems, they are faced with harsh and unrealistic expectations and images. Society is saturated with confusing messages: Be good but not too virtuous; be successful but don't break the glass ceiling; be accommodating even at your own expense. Society issues strong edicts to conform: Look thin; be popular; have the "latest," the "biggest," the "brightest." This image of who young women are supposed to be is at odds with reality. Is it any wonder that our daughters are confused, and consequently, are suffering?

"I like it when I get to drive my dad's Lexus," confesses Leah, an animated, smiling fifteen-year-old. "Kids that normally won't give me the time of day say 'hi' in the halls and talk to me at lunch. It seems more people want to be my friend and hang out with me. I know I shouldn't think driving a cool car is important, but it does make a difference." Leah realizes that having the "latest," the "biggest," the "brightest" should not matter. But her peers and society initiate and reinforce the message that appearances matter more than the person.

Mary Pipher documents this girl-poisoning culture in her bestseller, *Reviving Ophelia*. "Many of the pressures girls have always faced are intensified in the 1990s. Many things contribute to this intensification: more divorced families, chemical addictions, casual sex, and violence against women. Because of the media, which Clarence Page calls 'electronic wallpaper,' girls all live in one big town — a sleazy, dangerous tinsel town with lots of liquor stores and few protected spaces. Increasingly women have been sexualized and objectified, their bodies marketed to sell tractors and toothpaste. Soft- and hard-core pornography is everywhere. Sexual and physical assaults on girls are at an all-time high. Now girls are more vulnerable and fearful, more likely to have been traumatized and less free to roam about alone. This combination of old stresses and new is poison for our young women."

The world has changed for parents as well. Pipher goes on to say, "Parents have unprecedented stress as well. For the last half-century, parents worried about their sixteen-year-old daughters driving, but now, in a time of drive-by shootings and car-jackings, parents can be panicked. Parents have always worried about their daughters' sexual behavior, but now, in a time of date rapes, herpes and AIDS, they can be sex-phobic. Traditionally parents have wondered what their teens were doing, but now teens are much more likely to be doing things that can get them killed."

Ideally, it would be nice to change this toxic world, but realistically, this takes more time than you have to raise your daughter. Although society can be a scary place for girls, the point is not how bad the world has become, but that young women must learn how to adapt within this environment.

As parents, we must equip them with the skills they need to succeed within the existing world. We must give our daughters the tools to save themselves. The good news is that you can be the catalyst that positively changes your daughter's future. You can make a difference no matter where you are in your relationship — just looking for a little help with your daughter or feeling you might have lost her. Wherever you find yourself, you can learn to act with love and authority as the agent of positive change in your daughter's life. Your role as a parent cannot be underestimated. In his bestselling book *The Seven Habits of Highly Effective Families*, Stephen Covey clarifies this relationship, "The role of parents is a unique one, a sacred stewardship in life....[There isn't] really anything that would outweigh the importance of fulfilling that stewardship."

How you handle your parental job is vital during this formative time in your daughter's life. Your daughter is mastering the art of living, striving to become a successful, independent person. You are her master artisan in this world. She looks to you for guidance, structure, and love. She develops her mentality, methods, and morals under your influence. What her attitude is, what she does, and what she stands for all materialize in your workshop. Your daughter is your apprentice and your sacred responsibility.

Parenting during the teen years can be a painful and confusing time. As your daughter reaches adolescence, the necessary and inevitable growth toward independence escalates. Between the ages of nine and thirteen, your daughter will strive to lessen her dependence on you, until she ultimately becomes a responsible self-sustaining adult some ten to twelve years later. Your desire for control as your daughter struggles for independence complicates this relationship. If you concentrate solely on control, you will fail to help your daughter develop the skills she needs to become independent. You want your daughter to become a self-sufficient adult, but a little part of you might still want her to be a dependent child who needs you.

Jessica, a responsible fourteen-year-old from Kansas City, struggles with her mother for her increased independence. Sandra, her mother, a thirty-four-year-old single mother of two, admits she is overcontrolling at times, but justifies her tight rein as keeping Jessica safe. Jessica elaborates on the conflict, "My mom is a control freak. She wants to control everything about me, even what I wear. Last week, I asked to go to the mall with my friend Jenny to buy some clothes. Mom said that we could go on Monday. So, Jenny and I decided we would go after practice. But on Monday afternoon, Mom offered a lame excuse why she couldn't take us and said she would take me later. Who does she think she's fooling? I know she wants to take me shopping just so she can pick out my clothes. She treats me like I'm five." Jessica's feelings of frustration and anger are understandable because her mother is not hearing her plea for independence.

Sandra's feelings of protectiveness are understandable as well because she knows that a fourteen-year-old's lack of experience may result in poor judgment. However, Sandra fails to realize that her overcontrol is sabotaging Jessica's struggle for increased freedom. If she would allow Jessica small steps toward increased independence and responsibility, she could be less fearful in relinquishing her control, and her daughter could grow in responsibility. Initially, Sandra could allow Jessica to shop with Jenny while she is shopping in another department in the store. She could then meet Jessica to pay for the items, retaining the final say while letting Jessica have the freedom to choose her clothes. On the next trip, Sandra might drop the girls off for a short time and pick them up. Like Sandra, if you have trouble letting go, you may find the more you practice letting go in small steps, the easier it becomes. Incremental increases of independence and responsibility are the key to resolving this conflict.

Independence also can be an internal struggle for your daughter. She wants to grasp independence, but this means she must relinquish her dependence on you. She came into the world totally dependent on others for her care, development, and safety. Her feelings of confidence, security, comfort, and safety all were influenced by the quality of the care she received. Until now, she has thrived by relying on others to meet her needs, but this cocoon of security constricts the movements necessary for her growth.

Healthy self-esteem is a necessary component to developing independence. A positive self-image enables your daughter to take on more responsibility, achieving more autonomy. As she takes on more responsibility and independence, she sees that she has control in her world, and self-esteem increases. This symbiotic relationship is vital to her development.

Building self-worth is an individual lifelong process. As a parent, you cannot give your daughter self-esteem. She must do this work alone. However, you can create a workspace or environment conducive to healthy self-esteem. You also can impart strategies and encourage skills that will provide your daughter with the freedom to be a responsible, self-sufficient adult.

You can make the difference. The following pages describe how to provide a safe, secure environment where your daughter feels unconditionally loved and worthy. In this environment, she can explore the world with realistic boundaries and earn her independence. Within this cocoon of security, you can move with authority and love to help her develop decision-making tools and strategies that assist her in the arduous journey to adulthood.

Security: The Cornerstone of Her Foundation

"Home is a place not only of strong affections, but of entire unreserve; it is life's undress rehearsal, its backroom, its dressing room, from which we go forth to more careful and guarded intercourse, leaving behind us much debris of cast-off and everyday clothing." — Harriet Beecher Stowe

To develop her potential to the fullest, your daughter needs a safe and consistent family environment — a rock she knows she can depend on. As Cynthia Cooper, 1997 and 1998 Most Valuable Player for the Women's National Basketball Association, puts it, "The family is the rock; it has to be the rock. It can't be soft and change shape depending on how [your daughter is] doing in school, for example. It can't be something that transforms depending on how well she plays the basketball game. It has to be solid." Although you cannot develop self-worth for your daughter, security is a gift you can give her. Your daughter will face her challenges more confidently knowing she has a safe place to call home. Security in the home provides a foundation that allows your daughter to cope with new situations, expand her boundaries, and explore her potential.

You are still her safety zone regardless of your family's structure. Although there are varying definitions of family due to single-parent homes, remarriages, blended families, and working parents, the common denominator is the constancy of family support.

You can give your daughter security by providing assurance that you are there for her no matter what, through the good and the bad, even when things are not going well. When your daughter feels her world is crumbling around her, she needs to know that she can count on you. Knowing that you are always there helps her to come back to you, to trust you, to believe in you and the family.

At times you may feel threatened by your daughter's quest for independence. It may seem she is trying to distance herself from the family. In reality, she is not seeking separation from the family so much as an extension into the world. She needs to be able to move back and forth freely from the safety of her home into the sometimes scary world. She needs the security of her family to progress toward her independence. Family is her rock, her security, her cornerstone of support. When the family is her rock of security, she can increasingly gain independence.

As a parent, you should provide a safe, consistent environment for your daughter to acquire the autonomy and independence that she needs. This security is the cornerstone of your daughter's foundation of confidence and self-esteem. In a building, the cornerstone is the underground support system that ensures the integrity of the structure. Vital for a strong foundation, a strong cornerstone stabilizes the foundation and enables the structure to withstand the inevitable stresses and blows. The deeper and stronger the cornerstone, the stronger the foundation. Like the building's cornerstone, security is the substructure of support that enables your daughter to withstand life's stresses and blows. Parents, if you give your daughter a cornerstone grounded in love and stability, you are providing the ingredients necessary for a solid foundation.

Your daughter will need nuts and bolts to anchor her foundation or it will be shaky. You will need to love her no matter what and establish boundaries to build a secure foundation. These are the nuts and bolts of parenting that hold your daughter's foundation together, give it strength, and help her reach her fullest potential. Without them, her foundation will likely crack or buckle.

Tips from the Toolbox

Make a list of your daughter's attributes. Try to focus on her characteristics. For example, "My daughter is kind and generous" not "My daughter is a good basketball player." Remember, your daughter's self-esteem is safer when you focus on her as a full person, not just on her accomplishments in a specific activity or goal.

The Good, the Bad, and the Ugly:
Loving Her No Matter What

- -

"The one thing we can never get enough of is love. And the one thing we never give enough of is love." — Henry Miller

As a parent, your responsibility is to love your daughter through it all — the good, the bad, and the ugly. This love is independent of her thoughts, words, or actions. "Loving her no matter what" is absolute in its nature. You love your daughter not for what she does, or who you think she should be, but for who she is, flaws and all. Loving your daughter no matter what requires your acceptance, understanding, and action.

 Tips from the Toolbox

You may love your daughter no matter what, but does she realize this? Is she structuring her life based on what she perceives are your wishes, rather than her own? Is she blindly following your wishes (or what she perceives them to be), and in the process, betraying her dreams?

Talk with your daughter about her dreams and plans for the future. How can you help her get where she wants to go?

You are probably thinking that "loving your daughter no matter what" is easier said than done. You may also wonder how you can show consistent love and encouragement when you disapprove of your daughter's actions. Are there techniques that can help during these trying times? The answer is a resounding yes.

For many of life's trials and tribulations, there are simple strategies that work. You can't control every circumstance, but you can create a general feeling of acceptance and well-being for your daughter. During difficult and trying situations, your love for her and her sense of safety create the protective environment necessary for her strength and self-worth.

Loving your daughter no matter what provides stability during unstable times. When everything else is falling apart, the constant of this love offers your daughter a steady foundation of strength. No matter what she or the family is going through, love without conditions or qualifications provides the security she needs.

Even the most well-adjusted teenager will go through periods of self-doubt and insecurity. In this period of change and discovery, she needs the assurance of your unfaltering love. Your loving her no matter what tells your daughter that she is okay just as she is. When she realizes she is accepted flaws and all, she can then more easily accept herself uncondi-tionally.

LOVING YOUR DAUGHTER THROUGH IT ALL

Five things you can do to love your daughter during difficult times:

1. Separate the person from the action.
2. Allow a "bad day" to become an opportunity to be compassionate.
3. Never give up.
4. Stop worrying about what others think of you because of your daughter's actions.
5. Believe in your daughter's potential.

Author and well-known speaker, Zig Ziglar, in his national bestseller *Raising Positive Kids in a Negative World,* advises that words do make a dif-ference. He states, "The words and tone of voice you use with your children are tremendously important. Whether the words are loving and constructive or hateful and destructive can have a substantial impact on your child's life. Words do paint pictures, and the mind completes the picture." When parental judgments and criticisms are the focus, not only are they hurtful to the young woman, but they can be damaging. This constant, negative emphasis can color a young woman's perspective throughout her life. It can cause her to view the world as a hypercritical and demanding parent. If she internalizes this criticism, her inner critic will reinforce the message that everything she does is not good enough and the desire for an unachievable perfection will plague her. This may lead her to mistrust herself and find decision making difficult because of self-doubt.

Sixteen-year-old Keisha feels her parents don't understand her. Even though she makes good grades, she constantly worries about never measuring up to her parents' expectations. "I made four A's, a B, and one C in algebra last report card, and now all I hear about is the C. I can't have a spare minute without my mother or dad asking me, 'Why aren't you working on your algebra?' Do you think they even noticed the four A's? And they expect me to do all these extra things for my brother. I pick him up every afternoon from practice, and I watch him after school. But the other day, I was just fifteen minutes late. And Mom yelled at me. I get no thanks or anything for helping. It's always 'Take out the garbage, feed the dog, or put away the dishes.' Then when I finally have a minute to myself, it's back to 'Why aren't you working on your algebra?' Give me a break. Nothing I do will ever be good enough for them," she laments.

Keisha's parents have good intentions in assigning her responsibilities and are correct in holding her accountable. Although Keisha's parents probably feel they are doing everything they can for her, she only hears their criticism. She feels her parents are not satisfied with what she does do well. Keisha needs more from her parents.

In their hectic schedules, Keisha's parents have overlooked some simple techniques that can help Keisha feel more valued. Keisha needs to be praised for her good qualities, without her parents dwelling on her mistakes or short-comings. By curtailing the criticism and looking at the bigger picture, Keisha's parents can help her feel more appreciated.

Many parents grapple with how to correct their daughters without being overly harsh with criticism. Correction does not have to include criticism, but this trap is easy for parents to fall into. When your daughter only hears your criticism, it is difficult for her to know that you love her no matter what. The following tips, adapted from emotional health practitioners and teen psychologists, suggest ways for parents to embrace their teens and deal with everyday problems, while maintaining love and authority.

Instead of showing your frustration and anger and losing focus on what you want to accomplish when correcting your daughter:

■ Remain calm and picture yourself as relaxed. Use what works for you in managing your anger.

- Get in mind what you want to accomplish in dealing with your daughter. Keeping focused on the end result can take your mind off the heat of the moment. Your goal is to show your daughter her behavior is unacceptable, not that she is a bad person.

Instead of wrongly blaming others for problems with your daughter, or harshly blaming your daughter without compassion or understanding:

- Hold your daughter accountable for her behavior without judging her.
- Try to understand the reasons behind her actions and seek an appropriate remedy.

Instead of imposing an unrealistic image on your daughter, based on how you want her to be or how you want her to appear to others:

- Accept your daughter for who she is and help her see her potential.
- Consider your daughter's unique assets and value them.

Instead of judging your daughter as good or bad based on her behavior:

- Let her know she is not a bad girl, but her behavior is unacceptable.
- Be careful not to withhold love or affection based on her actions.

Instead of being too busy and self-absorbed in your own day-to-day activities:

- Make parenting your priority.
- Take the time necessary to be there for your daughter. It helps to remember that today is the only day you are assured of having.

Instead of only talking to your daughter when you must teach, instruct, or discipline:

- Tell your daughter you love her every day. A simple hug or a genuine "Glad to see you" goes a long way.
- Praise her positive attitude and desirable behaviors.

It is vital to let your daughter know you love and appreciate her. Your style and comfort level in demonstrating love are unique to your family and should fit your daughter's needs. Take these tips as a starting place for minimizing criticism and helping your daughter feel appreciated. There are many concrete ways to show your unconditional love.

Tips from the Toolbox

Parents, you need to present a united front when dealing with your daughter. Be careful not to let her pit one of you against the other. If you need more time to evaluate your response, ask for it. Be careful not to defer your authority and set up your spouse to be the fall guy in handling conflict.

Parents can inadvertently fall into the trap of conditional love. When you feel that your daughter should take a course of action for "her own good," your daughter can easily equate her personal worth with actions or characteristics. Denise, mother of three, is a prime example of this parenting mistake. Her daughter Emily is a well-rounded thirteen-year-old, talented in many areas including academics, athletics, and music. Emily's older sisters are both star volleyball players, and Denise was the top track star during her high school years. Denise desperately wanted Emily to follow the family legacy in athletics. When Emily decided to focus her efforts on her saxophone, she noticed her mother's subtle disapproval. Even though her mother attended most of her sisters' volleyball games, she rarely went to Emily's concerts and was often late getting her to band practice. One afternoon, Emily came home from school and overheard her mother telling her grandmother how disappointed she was that Emily was ignoring her athletic abilities and would miss the fantastic experiences her sisters had. Emily was crushed. She now understood the rejection she had sensed from her mother. At this point, Emily was in serious danger of internalizing her mother's thoughts and allowing them to damage her self-worth.

The great philosopher Aristotle helps to put Emily's thought process into perspective using his basic principles of logic. You probably recall the formula, which goes something like this: "If a, then b and if a, then c. If b, then a. Therefore, if c, then a." Emily's logic tells her: "If I am good, I feel good and if I am good, my mother loves me. If I feel good, then I am good. Therefore, if my mother loves me, I am good." Conversely (and where

Emily's thoughts have taken her), "If I am bad, I feel bad and if I am bad, my mother doesn't love me. If I feel bad, then I am bad. Therefore, if my mother doesn't love me, I am bad." When Denise withholds her love based on what she would like to see happen, she is telling Emily that when she "measures up" to her expectations, she loves her, but when she does not, she rejects her. Denise is using Emily's desire for her mother's love to control and manipulate her.

Loving your daughter no matter what means accepting her for who she is without control and manipulation. By doing this, you give your daughter the security she needs to expand her limits. (See "The Power Tool of Expanding Your Limits" on page 154.) Teaching her that she is worthy of respect and she is valued just as she is empowers her to take risks and resolve problems independently. As taking these risks meets with success, she builds feelings of competence and worthiness. And when she fails, your love gives her the confidence to try again.

As your daughter grows in this confidence of your unconditional love, her concept of love can develop to include self-love based on accepting herself just as she is. Your daughter's confidence that you love her no matter what helps her to build her own unconditional love and acceptance of herself.

Boundaries: A Working Partnership

"Build trust through telling it like it is and laying out clear expectations right up front." — Sean Covey

According to the *American Heritage Dictionary,* boundaries are the outermost line defining an area. In parenting, boundaries that work are realistic limits set to define the acceptable. Most people know that boundaries can help make a child's world more secure. Effective boundaries promote family harmony, add order to chaos, encourage accountability, and reduce crisis management.

However, you may not realize that boundaries can be a practical tool in improving your relationship with your daughter. On the next few pages, you will see how to set successful boundaries that create a win-win partnership between you and your daughter, improve communication, develop negotiating skills, and allow respect and trust to grow.

Building successful boundaries requires respectful, open communication from both of you. As you and your daughter learn to successfully negotiate the terms of the boundaries, you create a balance between her needs and your own. A working partnership can develop out of these negotiations. As you expand her boundaries, you can create a win-win relationship where your trust and her responsibility increase.

It may be a new thought for you to think of boundaries in terms of a partnership. However, boundaries work best and are easiest to enforce when structured as a partnership. By encouraging your daughter to participate in establishing her boundaries, you can increase the odds of her staying within them. Enforcing the boundaries then becomes easier because your daughter shares ownership of the guidelines.

Expandable, realistic boundaries offer the security your daughter needs to venture safely within her world and push the limits. Imagine a farmer planting a tree seedling. After carefully planting it, he wraps the trunk in burlap to protect it from insects. After a few years, the bark hardens and he removes the burlap and erects a small fence to protect the tree from animals. When the tree matures, the fence is no longer needed for protection. Just as the tree is protected from specific elements in its environment, your boundaries for your daughter will be specific to her environment. And just as the boundaries are removed as the tree becomes self-sufficient, your daughter's boundaries can be gradually expanded and eliminated as she grows.

Boundaries are not set in stone. They are unique to you and your family's values. All families do not share the same set of values or the same rules. Some families may use allowances as a tool to teach the importance of being competent with money. Others may emphasize the importance of schoolwork by making sure all homework is completed before their daughters can watch TV. You should consider your own values in setting boundaries with your daughter. When boundaries are in line with your values, they make sense and are easier to enforce. Talking with your daughter about your value system when structuring boundaries helps her to understand where you are coming from. It then becomes easier for you to create boundaries that incorporate your values and easier for her to follow them.

Your boundaries should also be specific to your daughter's surroundings and circumstances. Your daughter is not like anyone else, and therefore, her guidelines will be unique. For instance, one of your daughters may be fully capable of babysitting at eleven years old. However, your younger daughter may not be ready for this responsibility until she is thirteen. Only you know your daughter well enough to prescribe the particular boundaries that she needs.

Although individual family boundaries may differ, boundaries that work share similar qualities of

- Offering a child security through consistency and clear expectations.
- Improving both the parent's and the teen's reasoning and negotiating skills.
- Improving communication because they allow both the parent and the teen to know the limits and consequences of attitudes and actions.
- Being set by both the parent and the teen.
- Being flexible and expandable as the teen matures.

As your daughter assumes more responsibility on the road to independence, you will need to expand her boundaries to allow for her growth. Boundaries issued in love are for guidance, not for control. The goal is not to control your daughter, but for her to develop self-control. Boundaries should be structured to allow a gradual shift of control from you to your daughter.

 Tips from the Toolbox

A useful way to determine appropriate boundaries and limits for your daughter is to work backward. Imagine the time that your daughter will move away from home. What kind of decisions will she be making? What skills will she need? How can she get these skills? What kinds of experiences (mistakes) are necessary for her to learn all of this? Now, think about this and move backward to today. Structure simple steps that can lead her to her independence.

Consistency is the key to establishing successful boundaries. Your actions are more important than your words. If your daughter knows that you stand behind what you say and your guidelines are clear, your actions create security for her and minimize stress.

There are several common mistakes parents make in structuring boundaries:

1. **Some parents treat their daughters differently than their sons.** According to a survey by the Horatio Alger Association, an organization dedicated to understanding the opinions, views, and goals of America's youth, girls were twice as likely to have more rules to follow about dating than boys. You may find this to be true in your family. While you may feel justified in giving your daughter earlier curfews and more restrictions, be aware that you may be accidentally sending her a different message. She may not view these rules as protection, but feel that you trust her judgment less than if she were a boy.

2. **Parents often set boundaries that are too narrow.** This can prevent their daughter from developing necessary coping skills. Boundaries should not be designed to protect your daughter from the inevitable small blows and disappointments that every child must endure. Canadian researchers Stewart Page and Kathryn Lafreniere offer a simple example of a child caught at the top of a tree, shouting for help. Some parents wanted to climb the tree and get the child down immediately, while others encouraged the child to patiently make her way down. The parents who rushed to save the child robbed her of the satisfaction and the learning experience of handling the situation herself. The parents that let the child climb down the tree by herself chose to send the message "You can do it yourself" not "I'll get you down." They found that parents who held back and let the child help herself bred self-confidence. Your daughter must face challenges to develop coping skills. Adversity strengthens her character and makes her more compassionate.

3. **Parents set boundaries that are too broad without considering their daughter's developmental stage.** At the extreme, parents fail to set boundaries at all. Parents do this for several reasons:

because they fear or hate confrontation, they worry about being disliked, or they are too busy or lazy to enforce the boundaries. In reality, when parents avoid setting appropriate boundaries, they create an unstable environment where conflict is inevitable because no one knows the rules.

These mistakes all have a simple solution. First, you should consider your daughter's unique level of competency and adjust her boundaries accordingly. As she matures, her learning experiences may earn her an expanded boundary. You probably would not expect your sixteen-year-old to have the same curfew as when she was ten. Hopefully, she has increased in her understanding and abilities, and your trust in her has grown. As you consider her growth, it is important to note that individual developmental levels vary. What was appropriate for one of your daughters at a certain age may not be appropriate for the next. You as a parent know your daughter best and can determine her level of maturity when setting her boundaries.

> ### Mom's Memories
>
> Dennis Miller in his comedy routine on moms: "The relationship between mothers and children never changes, and that's because no matter how rich or powerful you are, your mother still remembers when you were three and put Spaghetti-Os up your nose."

The second part of the solution is to consistently enforce the boundaries once they have been established. The value of consistency cannot be underestimated. Clearly defined rules issued with firmness, reason, and love give your daughter the structure that she needs and help her feel secure in knowing her limits. Setting realistic, consistent boundaries allows your daughter to face her challenges more confidently and venture safely within her world.

Helen, an inner-city parent of two teenagers, relates how she and her thirteen-year-old daughter, Taylor, worked together to set boundaries. "Having been through one rocky teenage experience with Taylor's brother, Scott, David and I did not want to repeat the same mistakes with Taylor. We knew we needed to establish boundaries and guidelines for her before we faced the problems. So, one afternoon, we told Taylor we would like to set up a meeting to talk about rules and guidelines. We set a time that was convenient for each of us, when we would not be rushed or interrupted. In the meantime, we asked Taylor to be thinking about her needs and what she wanted. Before the day of the meeting, David and I sat down and listed our concerns about Taylor, and our values and goals.

"The night of the meeting, we all met in the kitchen with our note pads. We asked Taylor to tell us about her needs first. Boy, did she have a long list! Her repeated theme was her need for more freedom. At the top of her list were more clothes, later curfews, more understanding parents, et cetera. It was apparent to us that these needs were very important to her. We began to list our concerns about Taylor and our desire for her safety and happiness. We then told her about our values and why they were important to us. She listened intently and was not shy about her comments.

"Basically, what we came up with was a written list that included increased freedom and responsibility that was tied into her behavior. For example, doing the dishes for the week earned Taylor the privilege of going to a movie on Friday night. Both sides had to give a little, but we were able to reach middle ground that we both were satisfied with. Because Taylor had worked on the list with us, she had the necessary buy-in and the desire to comply. She even offered to type it up so that each of us would have a copy that we could refer to. It was not all smooth sailing along the way, but the agreement gave us a communication tool that opened our relationship with Taylor. And Taylor seems to have more peace of mind now and rarely presses the limits."

Helen and David found an effective tool in creating boundaries with Taylor. Their agreement illustrates many worthwhile elements that make boundaries successful. Some of these elements are included in the list below. You may find the following suggestions useful in setting effective boundaries with your daughter:

- Avoid conflicts by having clear, agreed-upon expectations up front. Structure the boundary so that both of you are satisfied.
- Negotiate boundaries with your daughter that include increased freedom and responsibility. These should hinge upon her behavior relative to your agreement.
- Evaluate her boundaries from time to time, and renegotiate the

terms if necessary. This will provide security and consistency that you both can count on.

A written list is one of many ways to set boundaries. You might prefer an oral agreement where nothing is written down, or a negotiated contract that includes signatures. Regardless of the method you use, successful boundaries will incorporate these specific elements.

Stephen Covey points out five elements in a win-win agreement in *The Seven Habits of Highly Effective Families*. Loosely paraphrased, they are as follows: Identify the desired results; set up the guidelines; make clear what the resources are; set up a system of accountability; and incorporate recognition and explanation of the consequences. Taking these steps is necessary for a successful negotiation. According to Covey, "The fact is, you are going to deal with these five elements sooner or later. If you don't choose to do it in leadership time up front (setting boundaries), you do it in crisis management time down the road."

Successful boundaries can be a superb tool in improving your relationship with your daughter. Respect and trust grow as you create this working partnership. Boundaries work best and are easiest to implement when they incorporate your value system and desired goals. By structuring and enforcing realistic and expandable boundaries, you are building a partnership with your daughter that you can enjoy for a lifetime.

Earned Independence: "Houston, We Have Liftoff!"

"No bird soars too high if he soars with his own wings."
— William Blake

When you establish a secure environment for your daughter, love her no matter what, and implement realistic, expandable boundaries, you create a formidable foundation for her. This foundation will be strong enough to be the launch pad from which she can successfully embark on the journey of life.

Launching your daughter into adulthood is a thrilling adventure. There is no greater joy than seeing your daughter successfully arrive at her destination — earned independence. Your primary objective as a parent is to gradually guide your daughter toward this goal.

The process to earned independence requires many years of shifting the control from you to your daughter. The key to mastering this parental shift is your awareness that this is the path toward earned independence, your ultimate goal for your daughter. There will be rocky places along the path, but when you remain focused on this objective, you can celebrate the successes along the way. Earned independence does not happen overnight, but joy is found in the journey. Letting go of your control will require all the courage and love that you can muster. Your awareness that letting go is a necessary and inevitable part of your daughter's growing up will make these years easier.

The thought that you cannot control another person, especially your own child, may be disturbing. However, the reality is you cannot completely dictate another's actions, but you can have influence. You have been the primary person your daughter looks to for guidance, boundaries, and love. Now her world includes other influences. While you still have an important place in your daughter's development, she now has other role models. It becomes essential that you do not overcontrol or abdicate your control.

Letting go means shifting control, not losing control. This shift requires time and hard work. Now is the time to ask yourself some important questions. What are the steps your daughter needs to take to accomplish independence? What does she need to learn now?

As your daughter shows increased responsibility, she earns the right to gain more independence. Then it is your turn to let go of your control proportionally with her increasing responsibility. Keep in mind that your daughter's independence is your goal and not your rigid control. You will probably find that the parenting style that once worked with your young daughter does not work when she is a teen.

Maintaining your relationship with your daughter will require a gradual shift in your method of parenting. This does not mean changing overnight. The shift that nurtures your daughter from dependency to self-sufficiency is a process that takes ten to twelve years. It can be a journey that takes leaps and bounds or a laborious trail of two steps forward and one step back. It is the overall progress that counts, not the setbacks.

Your responsibility shifts from micromanaging her every move to looking at the bigger picture. Once, she was dependent on you for all her needs. You managed all aspects of her life, deciding everything from her bedtime to her room color. Then, according to author Michael Riera, Ph.D., in his bestseller *Uncommon Sense for Parents with Teenagers,* "Without notification and without consensus you are fired from this role of manager. Now you must scramble and re-strategize; if you are to have a meaningful influence in your teenager's life through adolescence and beyond, then you must work your tail off to get rehired as a consultant.... Many of the adversarial aspects of the relationship stem from both parent and adolescent not understanding and appreciating this essential shift in roles."

Autocratic leadership, the exaggerated extreme of the micromanager style, can work, but it is at the expense of self-esteem. Historically, autocratic leaders such as Adolf Hitler, Joseph Stalin, and the Ayatollah Khomeini had rigid control over their people, and in the process, suffocated the individual. Their dictatorial style depended on a state of inertia that prohibited risk taking and independent thinking. This created a comfort zone, a seductive state, where it was easier for people to comply than to act on their own beliefs. Many found that as decisions were made for them, they lost their confidence to make competent decisions on their own.

When you choose a dictatorial micromanager style of parenting and never let your daughter question the "why" behind decisions, you rob her of life experiences that would assist her in attaining independence. When you fail to shift control to your daughter, you suffocate her sense of worth and trust in her own decisions. Parents can unintentionally take away the power their daughter has over a situation if they tell her exactly how to handle it. Most parents find that they can teach far more effectively by asking questions that guide her in the right direction rather than giving the solution away without any deliberation.

If you continue micromanaging your daughter's life, you will no longer be viewed as the caring, loving adult in her life, but as a manipulative, suspicious ogre. When you overcontrol your daughter's life, you send her the message that she is incapable of making sound decisions. She may feel that you do not trust her and that she is unworthy of your respect and love. You have rendered her powerless and damaged her capacity to make confident decisions.

If you continue this parenting style, you risk a fight or flight response. Your daughter may become angry and fight for control or become sullen and withdrawn. In either case, she probably will stop consulting you when she needs your help. This is a lose-lose situation for both of you. Your daughter loses by abandoning you as a valuable resource. She loses her self-confidence to make decisions and feels unworthy of your acceptance. And you lose your daughter's faith in you as a guide and an advocate. However, this lose-lose situation can be remedied.

You have the power as a parent to convert this losing battle into a victory. Early adolescence is the time to begin changing your parenting style to a consultant/monitor approach. As your daughter shows increased responsibility, you will need to let go of your control proportionally. By monitoring her progress, you can acknowledge her growth by giving her increased opportunities for independence. As she develops her decision-making skills, she can make more of her own decisions with you available to advise. This shows your daughter that she is capable of making sound decisions, which increases her self-trust.

 Tips from the Toolbox

Check your progress often in shifting from the micromanager to the consultant/monitor style of parenting. Assess where you are in the process and make necessary adjustments. Here are a few questions for you to use in evaluating your progress:

1. Have I given her enough (too much) freedom?
2. Am I letting her know what I expect?
3. Am I being consistent?

At first glance, it may seem that a person with true independence would not be accountable to anyone. In reality, these traits go hand in hand. True independence is earned. You must work to develop trust in your daughter's growing judgment, who in turn works to keep you informed of her developing responsibility. Using your daughter's increased responsibility to determine her freedoms can give you both a sense of great joy and accomplishment — and consequently, a win-win situation.

- When your daughter understands that you are letting her make these decisions, she discovers she has more influence in her world.
- As she shows more responsibility and competence, she will feel more self-assured.
- This realization gives her the freedom to consult with you, without fear of relinquishing her decision-making power.

By using the consultant/monitor approach, you support and encourage your daughter's decision-making ability, which will keep the door open for her to ask your opinion and maybe even take your advice.

Alyssa, a high school senior from Chicago, expressed to her school counselor how years of her parents' gradually shifting decision-making power to her has built trust and confidence in her relationship with her mother. "I knew selecting a college was going to be a difficult decision, but I really appreciate my mother's attitude. I thought she would push me into going to her alma mater, UCLA, but she surprised me. When I asked her about how it was at UCLA, she spoke frankly about the good and the bad. Although she asked me to look at the UCLA brochure and compare it to other schools, she actually wants me make up my own mind. I haven't decided yet where I will go to college, but I am relieved to know that whatever decision I make, my mother will stand behind me." Alyssa's relationship with her mother works because Alyssa talks openly with her mother about decisions she faces without fear of losing her mother's support. And Alyssa's mother feels confident that her daughter will make the right decision and is pleased with the respectful communication between them.

 Tips from the Toolbox

Save your power plays for when your daughter's health or safety is in jeopardy. Do you feel that failing a biology exam is on the same level as driving while drinking alcohol? If you treat small problems as life-or-death crises, she may not take you seriously when it counts.

When you switch to a consultant/monitor style, you might feel your role as a parent has diminished because you are giving up some of the decision making and control you once had. This does not mean you are dodging your parental responsibilities. Parental control is not about issuing a string of commands that your daughter may or may not obey. The control you think you have is not necessarily there. Ultimately, she still makes her own decisions. For instance, you might tell your daughter to come straight home after school. Your daughter decides whether to come straight home or stop at a friend's house. Whether she follows your request or not depends primarily on the influence you have in her life and what you have done to gain her trust. Real control of your daughter is the ability to continue to have an influence on her.

When your daughter asks for advice, you need to understand that she may have temporarily lost confidence in her decision-making ability and may need to borrow your belief in her. Many times, your daughter is trying to examine the problem and just needs to talk. By helping her sort out the details and not solving the problem for her, you can show your daughter that you believe in her ability to solve the problem. Then she will be equipped to solve the problem herself, and consequently, build confidence for future decisions she may face.

Gradually shifting control to your daughter builds her sense of personal power and responsibility. This provides an important foundation for the development of her self-worth and enables her to feel capable and confident. Having personal power means she has control over herself and is aware that her actions contribute to what happens in her life — what she does makes a difference.

DEVELOP LISTENING SKILLS

A good rule of thumb when listening to your daughter is:

- Look directly at your daughter. Put down the newspaper or what you are doing and look at her, intentionally letting her know she has your attention.

- Hear her words and the thoughts behind them.

- Let her know that she has been heard. Acknowledge what she said by paraphrasing or repeating her same words so she knows her point has been heard.

Twenty Strategies for Effective Parenting

Built on a cornerstone of security, your love and consistent boundaries provide the nuts and bolts your daughter needs to create a strong foundation that eventually becomes her launch pad into earned independence. Here are some strategies that can help to tighten these nuts and bolts and strengthen your daughter's foundation:

1. **Work on your own feelings of self-worth and help your daughter do the same.** Young women with high self-esteem usually have parents with high self-esteem. Encourage your daughter to develop a positive body image and healthy lifelong habits. Healthy habits and a positive self-image protect your daughter against the challenges she faces.

2. **Motivate instead of dictate to your daughter.** This will result in her freedom to control her own life and assume responsibilities and their consequences.

3. **Say what you really want.** Be careful not to give your daughter a choice unless there truly is a choice. For example, you might not want your daughter to go to a party. If you tell her you will ground her if she goes to the party, you have given her a choice of going and getting grounded. Actually, you meant to tell your daughter not to go to the party.

4. **Spend time together.** Quality moments have a better chance of happening when given more time.

5. **Develop effective decision-making skills and help your daughter do the same.** Let her make decisions when appropriate. Provide regular opportunities for her to choose. Follow through on your decisions and encourage her to do the same. However, if your daughter's health or safety is at stake due to some decision she is about to make, you will need to take control.

6. **Be careful not to send mixed messages.** Consistency is paramount for your daughter to feel secure. She can act with confidence when she knows what to expect.

7. **Help your daughter to realize the power and control she has in her own life.** Teach her to develop and rely on her inner guide. Let her know by your words and actions that mistakes are lessons on the path to wisdom.

8. **In problem situations, decide whose problem it is.** If it is your problem, solve it. If it is your daughter's, let her solve it whenever possible.

9. **Build your daughter's self-reliance by allowing her to do for herself** those things she can do, even if they are not done as well as you could do them. Be supportive without being too quick to help.

10. **Teach your daughter that there is dignity in hard work** whether it is performed with chapped hands over a sink or with the callused fingers of a musician.

11. **When talking with your daughter, have a conversation, an exchange of information or views.** "Go do your homework" is not as effective as saying, "What do you have for homework?" Then, *listen.* Listening makes your daughter feel valued. Your daughter may have things she won't tell you, but remain open. When she feels safe in talking with you, she is likely to tell you more. At times when you cannot devote your full attention but your daughter is ready to talk, it is important to listen. You may not have another opportunity.

12. **In giving praise, be sincere and specific.** "You're great" is not as effective as "You showed a lot of thoughtfulness calling your grandmother on her birthday."

13. **Showing your daughter respect** involves what you say *about* your daughter as well as how you speak *to* her. When you complain to others about your daughter or compare her unfavorably with another child, this damages her self-worth. There is nothing wrong with expressing disappointment to her when she does something that is out of line, but teasing or grumbling to others is quite hurtful as well as ineffective in eliciting appropriate behavior.

14. **Your daughter needs to know her feelings are important and normal.** An appropriate way to handle difficult feelings is to acknowledge them, then give her a little room. You can say, "Susie, I see you are quite frustrated with me. Why don't we both take some time to think through things?" When you acknowledge your daughter's feelings, she will feel valued and accepted.

15. **Acknowledge thoughts and ideas.** Ask your daughter what she thinks. You can learn from your daughter when you are open to hearing the answers.

16. **Make your daughter aware of her heritage and your traditions.** This heritage gives her roots of security and a grounded identity. Even simple traditions are fundamental in helping your daughter feel the richness and complexity of the family.

17. **Get involved.** Know what is going on in your daughter's life, who her friends are, where she likes to go, what she likes to do, and so on. Your interest will show your daughter that you care and help you monitor her activities.

18. **Don't take it personally.** Separate yourself from your daughter's actions. When she acts inappropriately, this is not a reflection on you. You don't need to take on her guilt.

19. **Model your values for your daughter about God, hard work, drugs, fitness, et cetera.** Stephen Covey, in *The Seven Habits of Highly Effective Families,* observes, "You cannot not model. It's impossible. [She] will see your example — positive or negative — for the way life is to be lived." Give your reasons for your beliefs and values and invite her to do the same. Make sure your walk matches your talk. When you model your values, you do not need to worry about preaching them.

20. **Be confident in your parenting ability.** You know your daughter better and care about her more than anyone else. You have the power within you to make the changes necessary for your daughter's growth.

TEN LIFE SKILLS FOR PARENTS

Each day, I will:

1. Realistically assess situations with a positive outlook.
2. Forgive myself and accept who I am.
3. Have an adaptable plan of action for my life.
4. Be open to new challenges.
5. Laugh.
6. Appreciate the blessings in my life.
7. Love my children through the good times and the bad.
8. Develop my spiritual self.
9. Take care of my body and mind.
10. Operate with honor and integrity.

Parenting does not have to be a war of clashing wills, continuous worries, and competitive wants. You can calm your conflicting wills, contain your ever-present worries, and synchronize your divergent wants by adhering to these tried-and-true techniques.

As a parent, knowing how to gradually relinquish your control can be confusing. You alone must decide how far and how much to let go. Keep in mind that eventually you will have to let go all together. It will be less traumatic for both of you if you do this incrementally. The consultant/monitor style of parenting works because it permits your daughter to assume responsibilities and experience the consequences. When parental control becomes self-control, your daughter becomes a responsible adult.

Despite the many challenges in today's complex society, your daughter can competently navigate the journey to adulthood. This chapter illustrated how you can give your daughter the security, love, and boundaries she needs to grow up in this world. But she needs more. Your daughter is launching into a life filled with awesome possibilities. She also will face life-altering choices. To face these challenges, she must build a strong internal decision-making center. Now comes the really exciting part. The next chapter describes this internal decision-making center, the master tool your daughter needs for her journey into adulthood — the Connected Inner Guide.

HONING THE SKILLS
What You Can Do

Understanding Her World — *This activity will increase your awareness of today's world and the different challenges your daughter faces.*

List what you liked about your teen years. What did you dislike? What could have made your teen years better? How do the memories of the challenges you faced compare with the challenges your daughter faces?

Creating a Loving Environment — *This mental exercise will help you get in touch with your values.*

How did you spend this past week? How important is the family to you? Do outside commitments often take you away from your family? Does your daughter view your home as her safe refuge? Think about the Cynthia Cooper quote on page 8: "[The family] has to be the rock." Ask yourself, "Is my family, marriage, home life the rock for my daughter?"

Establishing Realistic Boundaries — *This exercise will help you create a working partnership with your daughter.*

Consider what a win-win situation means to you. Think of a recent conflict with your daughter. What was the outcome? Did you walk away feeling good about the situation? Did she? Establishing a solution requires empathic listening and talking over options. When you work together, your solutions will be stronger.

Earning Independence — *This exercise encourages awareness of your ultimate goal for your daughter: her earned independence.*

What do you think is the ultimate goal of parenting? Do you recognize that your parental role is to help your daughter gain independence? How can you help your daughter earn independence? Review pages 21–26 for suggestions.

Review "Twenty Strategies for Effective Parenting" on page 27. Choose three of the strategies in areas where you would like to improve and put them into action.

What You Can Do with Your Older Daughter (Ages Thirteen to Twenty-Three)

Understanding Her World — *This discussion can help your daughter recognize the unrealistic expectations of society.*

Discuss with your daughter how women's desired body image has changed over the years. Does your daughter think today's stereotype of beauty is realistic? This skewed perspective of beauty is one of the reasons more of our daughters are becoming bulimic and anorexic. Now is a good time to discuss healthy eating habits and the importance of a positive self-image.

Earning Independence — *The path to earned independence often can be a rough and winding one. These exercises will help both of you in this journey.*

Earned independence is a two-way street. Both of you will need to work toward this goal. Set aside some time to discuss the meaning of earned independence with your daughter. Identify some of the things each of you must do to accomplish this.

Review the story about Helen and Taylor setting boundaries on page 19. Negotiate some written boundaries with your daughter and strive for a satisfying solution.

Have your teen write down some rules she would make if she were the parent. Explore her reasoning behind her rules.

Loving Your Daughter No Matter What — *Open doors to communication with these exercises.*

Ask your daughter if she feels you love her no matter what she does? Does she feel that you have placed restrictions on your love, and if so, when? It is important that you avoid being defensive as she responds. Be sure to listen with empathy and without judgment.

Review "Tips from the Toolbox" under "The Good, the Bad, and the Ugly: Loving Your Daughter No Matter What" on page 10.

Talk together about your daughter's dreams. How can you help her accomplish her goals?

Read the story of Keisha on page 12. Discuss some ways Keisha could have felt better about herself. What could Keisha's parents have done to help the situation? Ask your daughter if she has ever felt like Keisha. Help her identify workable strategies she can use when she faces a similar situation. What could you, as a parent, do to keep from repeating the situation?

What You Can Do with Your Younger Daughter (Ages Six to Twelve)

Comparing Your Worlds — *This activity promotes understanding.*

Cut out pictures from a magazine that depict how the world was for you as a teenager. Place these in an envelope. Now cut out pictures of how you think the world is for your daughter. Have your daughter do the same. Now compare the pictures and talk about the similarities and the differences.

Establishing Realistic Boundaries — *These exercises show both you and your daughter the difficulties of setting reasonable boundaries and the importance of working in collaboration.*

Pretend with your daughter that she is the parent and you are the daughter. Ask her to tell you what you should do this week and how you should manage your time. She should include what you should eat, where you should go, what you should do, whom you should see, when you should be home, and when you should sleep. Give her feedback, pretending to be the daughter. For example, if she has you getting up fifteen minutes before the bus comes, tell her you might miss the bus. Did she allow enough time for sleep, to get ready for school, to play with friends, and so forth? What did she miss because she didn't consult you in creating the schedule? Discuss the complexities of setting boundaries and the advantage of working together.

As a family, set up TV and Internet guidelines. Sincerely searching for realistic solutions is each family member's responsibility. As you develop the guidelines, keep in mind that the attitude of the negotiation, the give and take of compromise, is as important as the outcome. A win-win outcome will depend on negotiation.

Take your daughter to an all-you-can-eat buffet. Discuss with your daughter the choices she made and the limits she set for herself.

Loving Her No Matter What — *This game reassures you both of your love.*

Sit down with your daughter and play the "I Love You" game. Take turns finishing these sentences:

"I love you when you ___."
"I love you even when you ___."
Try to list at least ten answers, making a game of who can come up with the most.

Moving from Micromanager to Consultant — *This activity helps your daughter understand how your role as a parent has changed.*

Get out your daughter's baby book or some of her baby pictures. Talk with her about how she was as an infant and as a toddler. First, she needed you to feed, clothe, and change her. Later, she could feed herself, tie her own shoes, and go to the bathroom by herself. You no longer had to do everything for her. Note how your role as a parent changed as her needs changed. Today, her needs continue to change, but they are not as obvious as they were when she was younger. Ask your daughter to discuss with you her changing needs and to realize that you are trying to recognize her development.

Chapter Two

A HAMMER IN HER HAND
Making Decisions Using the Connected Inner Guide

"We stand at the crossroads, each minute, each hour, each day, making choices.
We choose the thoughts we allow ourselves to think, the passions we allow ourselves
to feel, and the actions we allow ourselves to perform.
Each choice is made in the context of whatever value system we've selected to
govern our lives. In selecting that value system, we are, in a very real way,
making the most important choice we will ever make." — Ben Franklin

Have you ever wondered what your life would be like had you made one decision differently? What if you had taken an alternate path or your timing had been different? Every decision you make has some impact, some consequence. Even a small decision has the potential to drastically alter the course of your life.

Adolescence is an amazing time, filled with countless opportunities and challenges for your daughter. She is facing many of the decisions that will shape her adult life. To successfully handle these potentially life-altering situations, she needs a strong internal decision-making center.

If you could give your daughter just one tool, it should be a basic skill to handle the challenges in life. Place in her toolbox the master tool that would augment her ability to make competent decisions: the Connected Inner Guide, the "hammer" of decision making. Depending on the decisions she makes, she will build up, tear down, or reshape the quality of her life. Properly used, this hammer of decision making enhances your daughter's personal power and strength.

Good decision making is a learned skill and must be exercised like a muscle to build strength. To help your daughter nail down good decisions, you must teach her to rely on her internal decision-making center. Positive growth and change require the development of this center that we call the Connected Inner Guide.

The Connected Inner Guide is a highly complex, integrated tool that provides the necessary wisdom and guidance to handle virtually every circumstance. Every decision your daughter makes is formed with this guide. This Connected Inner Guide is what she thinks, what she feels, and what she holds dear. It is a deep awareness and acceptance of who she is. The Connected Inner Guide, when functioning properly, builds your daughter's self-esteem. The Connected Inner Guide is the hammer that nails down control and strength in her life.

The Connected Inner Guide has three components — the head, the heart, and the gut — that shape sound decisions using an integrated approach. In this chapter, you will see how the head, the heart, and the gut work within the Connected Inner Guide. The next few chapters present strategies to strengthen these components and the effectiveness of the Connected Inner Guide.

Each decision-making component focuses on solutions in unique ways. The head offers discernment and options. In the thought process, choices are examined, rationally or irrationally, with deliberation. The heart offers a range of emotions. In the feeling process, options are affirmed or rejected with positive or negative emotions. The gut offers a personal evaluation based on values and universal principles. Within this instinctual component, right and wrong are measured. At its best, the Connected Inner Guide relies on a balance of the head, the heart, and the gut.

When left to their own devices, the head, the heart, and the gut have no desire for balance. Each of these decision-making centers pushes hard for control. When one component is allowed to dominate, it is at the expense of the other centers. The head wields reason and intellect to govern the decision making. The heart exerts emotions and feelings to justify its position. The gut exercises values and principles to prevail. Weakness in any of these components increases the power of the others, throwing the inner guide out of balance. To optimize the Connected Inner Guide's efficacy in decision making, these three components need to function in harmony and balance.

Harmony and balance are not the only elements that affect the proficiency of the Connected Inner Guide. The head, the heart, and the gut each impact the decision-making center based on how much influence they exert. Each component must be examined individually to fully comprehend their natures and their roles in the decision-making process.

- Within the head, there are competing inner voices that range from the Toxic Inner Critic to the Comforter. When functioning well, the Comforter affirms self-esteem and fosters good decisions. The Comforter uses reason to heal the wounds left by mistakes. At the other end of this continuum, the Toxic Inner Critic destroys self-confidence. This critical defeatist voice erodes decision making by instilling doubt and distortion. An awareness of the Toxic Inner Critic's distortions begins the process of changing this destructive force to the Comforter's voice. (This chapter discusses this component of the Connected Inner Guide in detail.)

- The heart has its own continuum of good to bad. The heart's emotions are indicators that affirm or reject available options. When functioning well, the Courageous Heart offers positive emotions to support appropriate decisions and negative emotions to direct inappropriate decisions. At the other end of the continuum, the Crybaby Heart's misuse of the emotions of fear, anger, guilt, blame, and envy prevents and misguides decisions. As the Courageous Heart intervenes, the Crybaby Heart is quieted. (See chapter 3 for more on the heart's contribution to decision making.)

- One's gut feeling or instinct is based on values that also fall on a continuum of good to bad. At the positive end of the spectrum, the Trained Conscience relies on both personal integrity and universal truths to influence decisions. On the negative side of the continuum, The Creep exudes little or no values. It is this void that alters decisions by its weakness in the conscience. The Creep is possibly the hardest component to change, but through perseverance, it can be retrained. The emergence of the Trained Conscience is vital to sound decisions and self-worth. (See chapter 4 for more on the gut's role in decision making.)

The Connected Inner Guide is perhaps your daughter's greatest tool. Every choice she makes shapes her life in some way. How well her Connected Inner Guide functions largely determines the quality of choices that she makes. You can help your daughter develop this tool by taking a closer look at how it works.

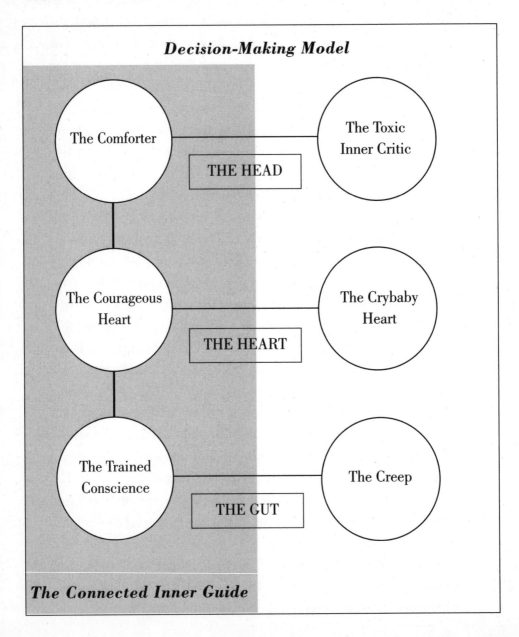

The Connected Inner Guide may be understood better by breaking it down into parts. You have probably seen a cartoon where a wise angel sits on one shoulder telling a bewildered man what he should do and an impishly grinning devil sits on the other shoulder giving different advice. These characters are the personifications of his internal struggle with choices. He can choose to listen to the angel and follow its guidance or succumb to the devil's advice. Just as the angel and devil are the cartoon personifications of the internal struggle with choices, this book gives the components found within the head, heart, and gut real character identities to better depict this internal struggle with choices. The Comforter, the Courageous Heart, and the Trained Conscience are like the angel — the positive influences on decisions within the Connected Inner Guide. The Toxic Inner Critic, the Crybaby Heart, and the Creep are like the devil — the dark, negative aspects that can influence a decision. All of us have a choice with each decision we make to either give in to the negative influences or overcome this dark side by employing the Comforter, the Courageous Heart, and the Trained Conscience. When these good aspects come together in balance and harmony, they become the Connected Inner Guide.

The Connected Inner Guide can be

THE GOOD NEWS ABOUT THE CONNECTED INNER GUIDE

The Good News:

1. The individual components of the Connected Inner Guide — the Comforter of the head, the Courageous Heart of the heart, and the Trained Conscience of the gut — can be improved.
2. These three decision-making components can be integrated for optimal results.
3. Properly employed, the Connected Inner Guide lends accountability, responsibility, power, and control to you and your daughter.

The Really Good News:

1. Both you and your daughter will improve your decision-making skills and the knowledge of who you are.
2. You will help your daughter to learn a life skill that can positively change every facet of her life.
3. You will deepen your understanding of your daughter and she of you.

understood, perfected, and customized as the master tool that creates strength and responsibility for your daughter. When you fully understand how the Connected Inner Guide operates to influence decisions, you can then teach your daughter how she can develop this life skill. Let's take a closer look at each of these components and then see how they work together to become the Connected Inner Guide.

The Head: From Critic to Comforter

"They can because they think they can." — Virgil

The head component of the Connected Inner Guide incorporates two character opposites that compete for influence. The positive character, the Comforter, is like a warm, snuggly satin quilt that envelops you in serenity and security and encourages confidence and responsibility. This mothering voice of support fosters accurate perception and evaluation. The Comforter's opposing character, the Toxic Inner Critic, is like a bloodsucking tick that drains you of confidence and vitality. It is a poisonous, fanatical voice of distortion and destruction. This chapter will divulge the secrets of the Toxic Inner Critic and expose its methods. As you begin to recognize its tactics, you can quiet its venomous voice.

Your Toxic Inner Critic tells you that you can't, that you aren't smart enough, that you aren't good enough. This toxic voice from within can destroy you from the inside out. The pessimistic Toxic Inner Critic thrives on guilt and blame and robs you of inner power. It strives to control your thoughts through intimidation and exaggerated distortions. Even when the Toxic Inner Critic tells you it is preventing you from making a mistake and embarrassing yourself, it is actually preventing you from experiencing necessary growth.

The Toxic Inner Critic at its subtlest can masquerade as a friend. Sarah, a thirteen-year-old student gifted in science and math, had an experience with her math teacher that is a prime example of this. When her eighth-grade algebra teacher tried to convince her to represent the school at the regional math finals, Sarah had reservations about going. In talking with her teacher, she was evasive and unable to come up with a reasonable excuse. Further conversation revealed that her Toxic Inner Critic was stealthily at work. Sarah voiced her fear that she was not very good at math, mentioning that she missed three problems at the last math competition. Despite her teacher's encouragement, she listened to her Toxic Inner Critic. The Critic convinced her by pointing out, "These competitions are tough. I know you'll miss some of the questions." This inner critic, in the guise of her friend, assuaged her fears with these thoughts: "I really don't want for you to be embarrassed. You don't need all of that stress anyway. I'll help you think of some reason not to go." By listening to and following the inaccurate advice of her Toxic Inner Critic, Sarah missed an opportunity to grow.

The Toxic Inner Critic, by its very nature, will create havoc on the other decision-making centers, ruin decision-making skills, and destroy opportunities for happiness and growth. Your daughter could have the other components of the Connected Inner Guide functioning well and still battle a Toxic Inner Critic that sabotages her decision making and keeps her from reaching her potential. The good news is that it is possible to help her redirect this critic into a positive voice from within. When she understands the conniving techniques of the Toxic Inner Critic, she can restructure the distorted thinking and ultimately rob it of its power. The Toxic Inner Critic uses several control techniques. The six distortions of the Toxic Inner Critic are

- Labeling — packaging the self into neat little boxes of predictability
- Tunnel Vision — seeing the world with blinders on
- All-or-Nothing Thinking — perceiving situations in black or white
- The Overinflated Self — overemphasizing one's importance
- Warped Control — feeling too much power or a lack of power in situations
- Mind Reading — assuming you know others' thoughts and they know yours

Tips from the Toolbox

Do you recall a time in your life when you really wanted to do something, but didn't, because a voice inside you told you that you couldn't do it and shouldn't try? Your daughter has this same inner voice. During adolescence, your daughter is hearing her toxic inner voice louder than she ever has.

You can help your daughter recognize when the Toxic Inner Critic is manipulating her decisions. For example, you might ask her why she didn't try out for volleyball or run for class office. Help her evaluate whether her response was due to this Toxic Inner Critic's influence. If she is reluctant to discuss this with you, you could tell her some of your own experiences with the Toxic Inner Critic. The first step to overcoming the Toxic Inner Critic is recognizing its voice and methods.

Labeling

"A great many people think they are thinking
when they are merely rearranging their prejudices." — William James

Labeling occurs when people internalize others' judgments or stereotypes. Labeling involves describing an event with language that is highly colored and emotionally loaded. Authors Matthew McKay, Ph.D., and Patrick Fanning, in their book *Self-Esteem,* suggest that you suspect yourself of labeling if the messages from your critic are perjurious clichés about your appearance, performance, intelligence, relationships, and so on. "I am stupid," "Blondes are dumb," "Girls are not athletic," or "Nobody in this family ever succeeds" are examples of the Toxic Inner Critic's use of labeling.

Society often plants distorted ideas in the head that the Toxic Inner Critic adopts and magnifies, reinforcing and exaggerating its skewed views. The Critic uses this labeling to categorize and squelch young women into conformity. Her Toxic Inner Critic devalues your daughter's self-worth and uniqueness with stereotyping and lies when it employs labeling.

One stereotype that girls might wear as a label concerns women's technology skills. A 1998 American Association of University Women study found that new gender gaps exist in areas like technology and career preparation programs. Only a very small percentage of girls take computer science courses even though 65 percent of the jobs in the year 2000 require technology skills. As long as women continue to wear labels of incompetence in these areas, they will shortchange their potential.

The more validity that girls give the Toxic Inner Critic's labeling, the lower their self-esteem. The lower their self-esteem, the more they listen to their Toxic Inner Critic. This self-destructive cycle feeds on itself, compounding the problem.

> ## RECOGNIZING THE CRITIC
>
> Recognize when the Toxic Inner Critic is present. Usually, it can be spotted when it uses one of these key phrases or thoughts:
>
> "She's just like all the other ___."
> "I'm a total failure. I never do anything right."
> "It's just like I thought."
> "They can't do it without me."
> "He should have known I needed that."
> "Why can't they see this is the only way it will work?"
> "I should ___," or "I must ___."
> "What can I do about it?"
> "Everybody will look down on me."
> "I'll make a fool of myself."

As many girls reach middle school, teachers find them less confident and unwilling to chance the embarrassment of answering incorrectly in class. This continues through high school as they "dumb down" to meet the expectations of their classmates. They must sort conflicting messages of what their peers expect of them that contrast with what they desire for their success.

For example, if a girl allows her Toxic Inner Critic to label her as bad in math, then when her teacher hands back a poor grade, the Critic reinforces, "Yes, I told you so." The next time the teacher asks her a question, even though the girl thinks she knows the answer, she doubts herself and chooses not to risk a wrong answer. The teacher assumes she doesn't know and doesn't call on her the next time. This reinforces the Critic's label, and the girl believes she is bad in math.

This "dumbing down" continues until it reaches crisis proportion in college when a young woman can face the competing message of being a successful career woman versus being the sweet, but not smart, teenage girl. Pressure to succeed, anxiety, and confusion all are results of this mixed message. If their Toxic Inner Critics are allowed to internalize society's competing labels, girls aim lower and achieve less than they should, and society loses the contributions our daughters might have made. Labeling also jeopardizes girls' ability to grow into responsible, confident adults. Society's stereotyping, backed by the Toxic Inner Critic's reinforcement of this labeling, packs our daughters into neat little boxes of predictability by the incredibly simple message "Conform and be accepted. Don't break the mold."

Tunnel Vision

"To often we ... enjoy the comfort of opinion
without the discomfort of thought." — John F. Kennedy

Using tunnel vision, the Toxic Inner Critic employs blind spots and selective thinking to assess situations. It ignores part of the situation and distorts reality. Tunnel vision is a method the Toxic Inner Critic uses to

1. Rationalize an inaccurate opinion
2. Justify an erroneous decision.

The Toxic Inner Critic employs tunnel vision to rationalize an opinion by narrowly focusing on a peripheral aspect of the situation and excluding the main factors. For example, it is probably human nature to blame one's problems on someone else. How many times have you seen a young woman blame the breakup of a relationship on the new girlfriend instead of her boyfriend or herself? Because she does not want to look at her own part in the breakup or view her boyfriend in a negative light, she deliberately chooses to blind herself to her own responsibility and blame the new girlfriend. By doing this, the Toxic Inner Critic can keep the young woman focused on the one aspect she cannot control and prevent her from realistically assessing the situation.

Tunnel vision can also distort competent decision making and may jeopardize safety. For instance, a preteen might ignore her parents' warning to wear a helmet while riding her three-wheeler over rough terrain. The Toxic Inner Critic justifies her decision not to wear a helmet by reminding her how much she likes feeling the wind in her hair and detests the discomfort of a sweaty helmet. Failing to look at the whole picture of safety and protection, she deliberately distorts the picture and allows her Toxic Inner Critic to endanger her life.

Our daughters can abandon their ability to make good decisions, but only by choice. Blind spots and tunnel vision are not accidents. They are not to be misconstrued as mistakes or lack of information. They are a deliberate attempt at distortion that will result in faulty decisions or conclusions. Until our daughters recognize that tunnel vision is impaired vision, their Comforter cannot direct their decisions with accurate perspective.

All-or-Nothing Thinking

"A mature person is one who does not think only in absolutes, who is able to be objective even when deeply stirred emotionally, who has learned that there is both good and bad in all people and all things, and who walks humbly and deals charitably with the circumstances of life, knowing that in this world no one is all-knowing and therefore all of us need both love and charity."
— Eleanor Roosevelt, *It Seems to Me*

All-or-nothing thinking distorts inner awareness by uncompromising, sharp, exaggerated positions. Your daughter can recognize all-or-nothing thinking by its black or white approach. There are no gray areas. There is only one correct way to do something in any given situation. And if this way isn't followed to the letter, then the action will fail.

The problem with all-or-nothing thinking is that your daughter inevitably ends up falling short of her expectations. No one can be perfect all the time, so at the first mistake, the Toxic Inner Critic falsely concludes, "If I am not perfect, then I must be a failure." This causes your daughter unnecessary pain and a loss of self-worth.

Another manifestation of all-or-nothing thinking employs the end-all-be-all philosophy: "It is my way or the highway." No compromise is considered. Even when it is obvious that neither A nor B is the perfect solution or even a good one, the Toxic Inner Critic won't allow any consideration of a middle-of-the-road alternative. All-or-nothing thinking dominates the decision-making process with unrelenting stubbornness. Being right supersedes doing right.

When used in making decisions, all-or-nothing thinking can lead to trouble. If your daughter fails to consider all the variables in the equation, she will lose perspective, and this may result in a faulty decision. All-or-nothing thinking is many times unrealistic. The head's Comforter knows the truth but the Toxic Inner Critic distorts the situation by reducing it to black or white.

 Tips from the Toolbox

Discuss with your daughter how hurtful all-or-nothing thinking can be. When you dig in your heels and refuse to compromise, positions become polarized and may result in undesirable outcomes. A good decision may require give and take.

Together, think about a recent confrontation. Did it result in a positive outcome? Did you let your Toxic Inner Critic use your stubbornness to have your way? Did you let being right supersede doing right?

The Overinflated Self

"If you are all wrapped up in yourself, you are overdressed." — Kate Halverson

The classic characteristic of the overinflated self is an exaggerated sense of self-importance. This distortion causes overcontrol. Thinking thoughts such as "I've got to make them listen" or "Nobody else can do it as well as I can" are clues that the Toxic Inner Critic is using this distortion.

Jean, a former president of a youth group, is certain the organization will fold without her continued leadership. Because she feels left out of the loop, she makes negative comments about the new leaders and how the group is being run. She constantly sets up conflicts where she can be viewed as saving the day. She has let her Toxic Inner Critic convince her that she is the only one that can effectively run the organization. Her undermining behavior causes organizational conflict and limits her growth. Jean's Toxic Inner Critic has created a false reality based on a distorted view of her importance. This is a classic example of the overinflated self, sometimes seen in teens who are leaders, but also in many girls struggling with low self-esteem.

The Toxic Inner Critic uses the overinflated self to alter your daughter's behavior by falsely thinking the whole world depends exclusively on her actions. This toxin of false ego obscures sound decision making and damages relationships with others. Author Ayn Rand, in her classic *Atlas Shrugged,* states, "The most selfish of all things is the independent mind that recognizes no authority higher than its own and no value higher than its judgment of truth." If your daughter feels that she is the only one who can adequately solve problems, she misses many opportunities to learn from others, to expand her perspective, and to appreciate others' abilities. When your daughter thinks that she is the only one that matters, there is no room for anyone else to matter. She risks damaging relationships because of her low regard for others.

Your daughter's lack of respect may be a symptom of her fear that others can do something better than she can. The overinflated self can cause her fear of inadequacy to evoke a reaction to present herself as superior. This superiority is a ruse. This distortion of the overinflated self can be a warning signal of underlying low self-esteem and is something to be aware of concerning your daughter's overall well-being.

Warped Control

"God, grant me the serenity to accept the things I cannot change; the courage to change the things I can; and the wisdom to know the difference."
— Reinhold Niebuhr, *Serenity Prayer*

With warped control, the Toxic Inner Critic can either overstate a girl's control and make her feel she must assume total responsibility for everything, or it can understate her control and make her feel that she is a victim. Warped control distorts a girl's perception of how much power she has in a situation.

Occasionally, you see an otherwise smart young woman dating a "bad boy." She is convinced she can change the boy into a better person just by loving him enough. Her Toxic Inner Critic tells her that her presence and support will cause him to reevaluate his behavior to become the person she thinks he can be. Even when he strikes her in anger, she continues to believe that she can change him. She twists the problem into being her fault and thinks if only she had done what he wanted, he would not have hit her. This naive teen's Toxic Inner Critic has warped her thinking into believing she can control others and it has put her at risk.

The other facet of warped control is lack of control, or understating the amount of power a person has in a situation. This victim mentality is a lie that the Toxic Inner Critic uses to distort thinking. The conspicuous characteristic of this technique is the prevailing attitude, "What can I do about it? My hands are tied." Underlying this attitude is the comforting thought, "How could I be to blame? I have no control over the situation."

Control or lack of control is a gnawing distortion that alters accurate perceptions. Attempting control where you have no control is like trying to hold on to beach sand. The tighter you hold on, the more it slips through your fingers. Your daughter needs to understand that true control means being responsible for her own thoughts and actions.

Mind Reading

"I know you think you thought you knew what you thought I said, but I'm not sure you understood what you thought I meant." — Anonymous

Everyone is familiar with mind reading as entertainment, an old trick employed by magicians to entertain audiences. However, few recognize it as a technique that the Toxic Inner Critic uses to distort thinking and assimilate false information. Mind reading typically occurs in two ways: expecting others to know your thoughts, requests, or needs without conveying them and assuming you know others' thoughts without being told.

Here's an example of the first form of mind reading, that of assuming others know your unspoken thoughts: Emily expects her mother to come to her after-school basketball practices. However, Emily doesn't ask her mother to come because she assumes that her mother knows she wants her there. The fallacy of this thinking is that Emily assumes her mother thinks like she does on this issue. If Emily has not made her thoughts, requests, or needs known, then how can her mother know what she expects?

On the other hand, trying to figure out what others are thinking wastes time and can be misleading. When a friend doesn't call, a young girl might think that her friend does not care or is angry. The next time she sees her friend, the girl is cold toward her, and this puts her friend (who previously was not angry) on the defensive. This incident reinforces the young girl's initial miscalculation that the friend was angry. The original false premise becomes a self-fulfilling prophecy as it feeds on itself to become a true assumption. The girl inaccurately concludes that her initial hunch was right, which reinforces the Toxic Inner Critic's power in this distorted thought. Many young women unwittingly embrace the Critic's philosophy that mind reading is one of the necessary requirements for any relationship and they fail to see its destructive effects.

 Tips from the Toolbox

Sit down with your daughter and list three assumptions she made about you this past week and three that you made about her. Were they accurate assumptions? Did you jump to any conclusions? Point out how the Toxic Inner Critic can lead to false conclusions.

Mind reading is a cognitive disorder that damages the power to reason by leaping to conclusions without any real evidence. It is a diversion to avoid facts by giving perceptions more power than the truth. Mind reading distorts the facts by projecting artificial constraints or beliefs that color the outcome of the situation.

The distortions of labeling, tunnel vision, all-or-nothing thinking, the over-inflated self, warped control, and mind reading all omit necessary information that is needed to make competent decisions. The Toxic Inner Critic uses these distortions because it desires to be in control. However, this is at the expense of the other components of the Connected Inner Guide. The Toxic Inner Critic wreaks havoc on the Comforter within the head, and on the heart and gut when it is given too much power.

Some girls may not recognize that they even have a Toxic Inner Critic. One mother, Jacki, was adamant that her daughter, Rachel, did not have an active Toxic Inner Critic. She described Rachel as extremely confident and poised. She was on the debate team, made good grades, and excelled in gymnastics. Rachel had a large circle of friends and was always outgoing. However, when Jacki put her assumption to the test, she was surprised. She asked Rachel if she had an inner voice that ate away her confidence. Rachel replied no and went on to say she rarely let criticism get to her. So, Jacki took it one step further and said, "What if I said I thought you weren't very good at gymnastics (an activity Rachel always excelled in)?" Rachel immediately responded, "I know. I know. I can't seem to get any of my floor exercise down." Jacki was astounded at how quickly Rachel internalized her comment that was not even true. Jacki quickly told Rachel how good she thought she was in gymnastics and that she did not mean for this comment to be taken literally. As Jacki discovered, even the most confident girls can have an active Toxic Inner Critic that undermines their self-worth.

The Toxic Inner Critic negates positive feelings and rational thoughts that cushion difficult times. During these difficult times, it convinces our daughters that it is acting as a friend to spare them from pain and suffering. As a personification of our daughters' mental state, the Toxic Inner Critic is not as concerned with our daughters' welfare as it is with its own preservation and control. It knows its healthy counterpart, the Comforter, is battling just as hard for control in the head. The Toxic Inner Critic's power is in danger when sound reasoning and good judgment prevail. The good news about the Toxic Inner Critic is that your daughter can choose to give it power or not. She is equipped with a Comforter that can disarm her Toxic Inner Critic and nail down sound decisions.

Disarming the Critic by Listening to the Comforter

"It's hard to fight an enemy that has outposts in your head." — Sally Kempton

On the head component's continuum of good to bad, the healthy inner voice of the Comforter can be just as effective as the Toxic Inner Critic in influencing decisions. Your daughter must learn to listen for the Comforter's voice and to apply the strategies that the Comforter uses to make good decisions and overcome the Toxic Inner Critic. As your daughter learns to develop and rely on her Comforter, she empowers the Comforter as her decision maker and reduces the power of the Critic.

To combat the Critic effectively, your daughter needs to listen to her Comforter. David Burns, M.D., in his book *Feeling Good*, recommends three crucial steps to combat the Critic's distorted thinking:

1. Zero in on negative thoughts and write them down. Don't let them buzz around in your head; capture them on paper.
2. Read over the list of cognitive distortions. Learn precisely how you are twisting things and blowing them out of proportion.
3. Substitute a more objective thought in place of the distorted perception. As you do this, you'll begin to feel better.

Just as the Critic has its techniques to undermine self-worth, the Comforter has effective responses to combat the Critic and empower good judgment. The Comforter, your daughter's healthy inner voice, is her most effective ally, friend, coach, advocate, and healer.

As her ally, the Comforter protects your daughter from the Critic's stinging barbs. Suppose your daughter's Toxic Inner Critic tells her, "Everybody else is going to the party but you. You are obviously not popular enough for that crowd. You are such a loser." The Comforter as her ally rushes in to protect her. The Comforter points out that her friend Janie is not going and suggests that she call her and invite her to a movie. The Comforter refutes the Critic's damaging exaggerations and offers solutions that bolster her perspective.

As a friend, the Comforter points out that the Critic is not her buddy. The Comforter boosts confidence by reminding her of her good points when the Critic badgers her. For example, when the Critic calls her a loser, your daughter's Comforter responds, "You know better than that. You have some quality friends that like you for who you are." Your daughter can disempower the Critic and dispel her doubts when she learns to listen to the Comforter's voice.

As your daughter's coach, her Comforter maps strategies to defeat the Critic. For example, her Comforter may rebut the Critic with this plan: "The next time your Critic jumps in and says you are stupid because you got a bad grade in math, you tell it about all your good grades from the rest of your classes. Besides, you've been working hard on your word problems, and I know you will do well on the next math test." The Comforter is committed to helping her win.

As her advocate, your daughter's Comforter skillfully pleads her case. This advocate uses reason and logic to argue against the Critic. When the Critic tells your daughter to try marijuana and that everybody else is getting high, the Comforter points out truths in the situation, "You're talking illegal here. Wait a minute. Not everybody is doing it and it could be harmful to your health." The Comforter as an advocate secures sound judgment against the Critic.

As her healer, the Comforter

> ## TALK BACK TO THE TOXIC INNER CRITIC
>
> When your Toxic Inner Critic begins to undermine your thoughts, disarm it with one of these commands:
>
> "This is not healthy. Stop it!"
> "No more put-downs."
> "Quiet!"
> "I am not going there."
> "Nonsense. I do a lot of things well."
> "These are lies."
> "Come on. Ease up. I'm not a jerk."
>
> Any of these phrases can help you start to disarm the Critic. Use what works for you. Sometimes, one phrase can debunk the Critic. At other times, you will need to have a lengthy dialogue with it.

compassionately treats her wounds and assuages her hurt feelings and negative attitudes. When the Critic does succeed in harming your daughter, her Comforter soothes her by saying, "You are still a good person. You just made a mistake. We'll learn from it and move on." The Comforter bandages the abrasions and removes the toxins left by the Critic.

Sometimes, the Comforter may silence the Toxic Inner Critic merely by recognizing its manipulative distortions. More often, though, recognition is just the first step in combating this toxic voice. Depending on the circumstances and what works best for your daughter, she may need different responses, or a combination of these responses. Her Comforter assumes roles as her ally, friend, coach, advocate, or healer to overcome the Critic. Your daughter's trust in the Comforter increases as she learns that her Comforter is always there for her.

Ten Strategies to Overcome the Toxic Inner Critic

Recognizing and disarming the Toxic Inner Critic's distortions will help your daughter replace negative thoughts with the rational thought process of the Comforter. As your daughter masters these techniques, she will gain control and confidence. Below are some strategies that can help her quiet her Toxic Inner Critic:

1. **Avoid reinforcing labels.** Ensure within your home that you are not reinforcing any labels for your daughter, such as "She's the bright child" or "She's the athletic one in the family."
2. **Value individuality.** Marching to the beat of a different drummer is okay. Be accepting.
3. **Avoid placing limitations on her potential** by making statements such as "You might not become a doctor, but you could be a nurse." This places an artificial ceiling on what she can achieve.
4. **Encourage pragmatic optimism.** Realistic positive perceptions empower a person no matter what the circumstances.

5. **Remove the blinders of tunnel vision** and look at every factor that caused the situation. Help your daughter recognize when she is not looking at the whole picture. She should make a decision based on all the facts.

6. **Be careful not to send your daughter the message that she is the center of the world.** Help her to see how her life intertwines with her family, her community, and the rest of the world. Encourage altruistic activities to help her gain a generous perspective.

7. **Learn the art of compromise.** When faced with a problem, write down all possible solutions, even the unlikely ones. This can help to open your daughter's mind to other alternatives she may not have thought of.

8. When your daughter finds herself thinking that she can do nothing, she should take another look. Point out to her that feeling a lack of control is rarely an accurate assumption. Tell her and show her that **you always have control over one thing — your attitude.**

9. Perfectionism is man's ultimate illusion. Don't expect your daughter to be perfect. Be accepting when she makes mistakes. This will show her how to **love herself, flaws and all.**

10. It is important for your daughter to **believe her rebuttals** to the Toxic Inner Critic. She may not be successful at first, but the more she practices, the stronger her Comforter will be. (For more ways to overcome negative thinking, see "How to Make Mirror Talk More Effective" on page 56.)

Within the head, the Comforter directs and governs with sound truths and dependable reasoning that are vital to survival and happiness. It protects and pilots, nurtures and comforts. The Comforter is indispensable in keeping our daughters in line with their goals and values throughout life.

The Comforter is the key element in overcoming criticism from any outside source. When the Comforter is functioning well, our daughters can take responsibility when they are at fault and deflect inaccurate accusations. Eleanor Roosevelt once noted, "Nobody can make you feel inferior without your consent."

By examining how the Comforter handles criticism from others, the strength of this inner voice becomes apparent. When the Toxic Inner Critic is booming commands out of misdirected perceptions, the real-life critics in a young woman's life become more powerful. If the critic is a parent or person of importance, criticism may become a focal point to internalize self-hatred for perceived shortcomings. Twelve-year-old Kaitlyn, reluctant to smile because of braces on her teeth, had just moved out of state to a new junior high school. Her gangly physique kept her from standing up straight and she found it difficult to make friends because of her shyness. Her confidence at this stage was, at best, fragile. Unsurprisingly, Kaitlyn began to feel like an outsider in her new school. One day, she overheard several girls in the hall making fun of her appearance. Her Toxic Inner Critic immediately picked up on their criticism and magnified the pain she felt. Weeks passed with Kaitlyn becoming more and more miserable. Finally, Kaitlyn tearfully told her mother about the girls' critical remarks and her feelings of exclusion. Her mother understood the Toxic Inner Critic's techniques and the pain that the Critic had caused. She showed her daughter that the way Kaitlyn internalized the remarks caused her pain. She helped Kaitlyn see that her attitude was a choice. Kaitlyn could overcome these feelings of inadequacy by listening to her Comforter. Her mother suggested some consoling thoughts that her Comforter could use to defeat the pain of the Critic. She reminded Kaitlyn that real friends will like her for who she is. Together, they made a plan for Kaitlyn to meet some new friends at school. Kaitlyn's critics became less powerful in her life as she let her Comforter come to her rescue.

Observing the external critics and situations children endure gives clues to the fortitude required to overcome the Toxic Inner Critic. The Toxic Inner Critic can be converted to the comforting salvation of a healthy inner voice. From Critic to Comforter, the inner voice of a young woman must grow to align with her values, faith, and sound judgment. The toxicity can rear its ugly head at times, but will gradually shrink as the young woman repeatedly takes the reins of confidence and acts according to her healthy inner voice. As the Comforter takes charge, the young woman will increasingly gain wisdom and peace. The Comforter wins.

There are many positive benefits for your daughter when she learns to listen to her Comforter. Replacing negative thoughts with positive ones bolsters her self-esteem. Using the rational thought process of the Comforter improves her decision making. She is empowered to move forward with confidence and not be crippled by her Toxic Inner Critic. The turmoil that the Toxic Inner Critic caused is quieted, resulting in her peaceful acceptance of the situation. And best of all, responsibility and control are returned to her.

To describe further how sound decisions are made, we'll examine the other two components of the Connected Inner Guide, the heart and the gut, in the next two chapters.

HONING THE SKILLS
What You Can Do

———————————————————

Understanding Your Daughter's Toxic Inner Critic — *This mental exercise will offer you a perspective on the challenges your daughter faces with her Toxic Inner Critic.*

> How does your Comforter handle your Toxic Inner Critic? What techniques do you use to quiet negative thoughts? Recall how your Toxic Inner Critic reacted when you were a teen. Was your Comforter as adept as it is now at handling your Critic's challenges? How much of your Comforter's strength is due to your experience level and amount of knowledge? Remember, your daughter does not have the benefit of experience to help to overcome her Critic.

Modeling Your Comforter — *This ongoing activity is extremely important for your daughter to fully implement her own Comforter.*

> Your opinion of yourself, how you view the world, and how you react to situations all have a tremendous impact on how your daughter chooses to view herself and her position in the world. When you allow your Critic to put you down and make you feel you have no power in situations, your daughter is watching and learning. When you realize you are letting your Critic control you, discuss with your daughter your mistake and your plan to correct it.

What You Can Do with Your Older Daughter (Ages Thirteen to Twenty-Three)

Recognizing the Critic — *This exercise will help dispel the power of your daughter's Toxic Inner Critic by identifying its techniques.*

Help your daughter realize the underlying motives of her Toxic Inner Critic. When she understands her Critic's ulterior motive, to destroy confidence and esteem, she can feel less vulnerable to it. The only way the Critic's attacks are successful is when she believes and reinforces them. When she can identify the role her Critic plays, she can better assess the credibility of its message.

When your daughter's Toxic Inner Critic is tormenting her, encourage her to write the distortions down and counter them with the truth. If your daughter is struggling with feeling inadequate, ask her to be very specific about her shortcoming. This will make it easier to debunk the distortion with a positive comeback.

What Would Your Comforter Do? — *This game will create an awareness and stimulate thinking about ways to overcome the negative inner voice.*

Several times a month, play a game with your daughter called "Catch the Critic." (This may be a game the whole family would enjoy.) Play each scenario out using the different roles of the Comforter: ally, friend, coach, advocate, and healer. After you complete these scenarios, think of your own. As you become adept at these, throw in some real-life experiences.

Here is how to play: For each of the scenarios, answer the questions that follow.

Scenarios:
1. You are not invited to a friend's party.
2. You did not make the team.
3. You want to go to a movie. Your parents say no.
4. You are afraid of heights.
5. You are overweight.
6. You forgot your best friend's birthday.
7. You decide to run for class president.

Questions:

What would your Toxic Inner Critic say?

How would the Comforter as your *ally* conquer the Critic?

What good points about you would your Comforter as your *friend* recall?

What strategies or exercises would your *coach and trainer* have you try to help you win?

What reasoning and logic would your *advocate* use to argue against the Critic?

How would your *healer* treat your wounds?

What You Can Do with Your Younger Daughter (Ages Six to Twelve)

Understanding Her World — *This exercise will help your daughter spot negative stereotyping and help discourage it.*

> Jokes that stereotype a group of people are harmful in perpetuating a false image. Whether it is a racial, ethnic, or "dumb blonde" joke, the Toxic Inner Critic delights in reinforcing this labeling. Help your daughter think of a strong reply or action that shows her disapproval. The circumstances may vary and her reaction will need to be appropriate. If she is in a meeting and a speaker tells a joke that puts down a group of people, she might find it more effective to wait and talk with the speaker after the meeting. If she is with a few friends, she might stop the joke and say that it makes her uncomfortable to put down a group of people. At other times, she may just simply walk away. By doing this, she will empower her Comforter to resist labeling.

Gaining a Broader Perspective — *This activity will help your daughter to encourage selfless motives.*

Talk about the overinflated self and how damaging it is to self-worth. Plan a family day where you go together and volunteer at a community charity. Select a food pantry, a homeless shelter, a children's home, a nursing home, a free clinic, et cetera. Working with those in need takes away the emphasis on self.

Chapter Three

FROM CRYBABY TO COURAGEOUS

The Heart's Role in Making Decisions

"Some people carry their heart in their head and some carry their head in their heart. The trick is to keep them apart yet working together." — David Hare

Literature and art abound with works about the heart and its role in enhancing life. Throughout history, man has depicted the heart as a guiding force. Poets, novelists, and musicians have lauded and lamented its passion. Artists have used many phrases to illustrate the significance of the heart: "Follow your heart," "Take it to heart," "Don't lose heart." A stone-cold heart, a bleeding heart, a broken heart — what feelings do these phrases evoke in you? For many, these expressions are fraught with powerful feelings. They illustrate the enormous role that the heart plays in decision making and one's outlook on life.

The heart is a major force in the direction and the strength of the choices your daughter makes. Her Connected Inner Guide relies on her heart to balance the decision-making process with her head and her gut. These three components must work together to generate sound decisions.

Each of these components of the Connected Inner Guide focuses on making decisions in different ways. While the head contributes reason and intellect to the decision-making process and the gut offers a personal evaluation based on values and principles, the heart supports its position with emotions and feelings. Together, these three components create a decision-making tool that is invaluable to your daughter. In chapter 2, you saw how the first component of the Connected Inner Guide, the head, influences decisions within the thought process. Now, let's examine the second component of the Connected Inner Guide, the heart.

Just as the head has positive and negative character opposites (the Comforter and the Toxic Inner Critic that battle for control in decision making), the heart also has its competing forces, the Courageous Heart and the Crybaby Heart. These opposing forces depict the heart's internal struggle with choices. The heart as a decision-making center has desirable emotions like happiness and gratitude, as well as dark, negative feelings that battle for control.

The Crybaby Heart would have you believe that emotions happen to you and you have no control over them. This is a fallacy. Emotions can be trained and controlled. The Crybaby Heart can dominate decisions with destructive and exaggerated emotions but the Courageous Heart can keep these emotions in check, leading to a sound decision-making center within the Connected Inner Guide.

Each day, each hour, each minute, the heart experiences a myriad of emotions. However, some emotions are particularly toxic for our daughters. Envy and blame are two of the deadliest poisons the Crybaby Heart uses, primarily because they cannot be easily redirected.

Erin, an energetic, talented high-school freshman relates how envy and blame almost ruined one of her closest friendships. Erin and her best friend Vonda both really wanted the lead part in a school play. When the auditions were completed and the cast list was posted, Erin was disappointed to see that the lead part was given to Vonda. Erin describes her feelings, "At first, I felt like crying. Vonda knew how badly I wanted that part, but she didn't care. She jumped up and down squealing and hugging and high-fiving everybody. I felt so betrayed. I couldn't believe my best friend could do this to me. In the car on the way home, I said some really mean things to her. Now, thinking back, I realize it wasn't her fault. But at the time, I let my envy get in the way. Now she won't even speak to me. And to make matters worse, I didn't go back and try out for another part. I wish I had taken the time to think it through. Now I'm not in the play at all and I may have lost my best friend." Erin made several poor choices because she let her Crybaby Heart focus on several negative emotions. While it was normal for Erin to feel envy, anger, and blame, problems arose when she acted upon these destructive emotions.

The Crybaby Heart uses emotions such as envy, fear, guilt, and anger to distract the heart and paralyze decision making. However, the Courageous Heart can redirect these emotions, and they can become useful indicators to make sound decisions and produce appropriate behaviors.

The Courageous Heart must battle the emotions of the Crybaby Heart because these emotions skew perspective. To accomplish this, the Courageous Heart must realign emotions such as fear and guilt, manage anger, and defeat envy and blame. Then, the power of happiness and gratitude, combined with forgiveness and compassion, can equip the Courageous Heart to overcome the Crybaby Heart.

Each of the Crybaby emotions is particularly toxic because of the damaging effects they have on your daughter's heart as a decision-making center. Learn to recognize when these negative emotions are wielding too much control:

- Insatiable Envy — jealousy that deceives and consumes
- Deflective Blame — lambasting others to dodge responsibility
- Paralyzing Fear — an indicator of danger or an inhibitor of action
- Mismanaged Anger — overreacting with displeasure or hostility
- Inappropriate Guilt — a remorseful awareness of wrong

Insatiable Envy

"Envy is as persistent as memory, as intractable as a head cold." — Harry Stein

An old German proverb states, "Envy eats nothing but its own heart." Envy is a gnawing and deceptive emotion because it leads to a perpetual feeling of discontent. If you take a closer look at this green-eyed monster, the underlying causes of envy are revealed and much of its power is lost.

Envy can take different forms in the Crybaby Heart. One form of envy is jealousy for another's possessions. Another form of envy is the feeling of inadequacy when comparing oneself to another. Philosophy professor Joshua Halberstam, in his book *Everyday Ethics*, notes, "Envy is a demeaning emotion. Why is envy demeaning? Because it highlights what we want but don't have." Whether they like it or not, our daughters are constantly being compared to their peers. As seniors in high school, they are given a class rank; in band, they try out for the number one chair and are positioned in order of skill; in sports, they make the A, B, or C team, depending on their performance. No matter where our daughters turn, they are constantly reminded how they measure up to others. The Crybaby Heart can internalize these comparisons and see the self as inadequate, which often results in envy. This envy can cause our daughters to have a perpetual feeling of discontent with their circumstances, and more important, with themselves.

Unlike all other emotions, envy never feels good. Halberstam goes on, speaking of the green-eyed monster, "Envy offers no joy. No one relishes the pangs of resentment and inferiority that accompany it." Envy is painful even when only experienced mildly. Envy eats up space in your daughter's heart, leaving a bitter taste. It devours the positive emotions of the Courageous Heart. Happiness and gratitude are poisoned by the rancid emotion of envy. If your daughter's Crybaby Heart embraces this driving emotion, she enhances its power. It is impossible for your daughter to feel good about herself if her Crybaby Heart harbors the toxin of envy. This caustic emotion will destroy her inner feelings of positive self-worth.

Because envy is such a destructive emotion, it is crucial that the Courageous Heart recognize and defeat it. As with most problems, it is easier to correct envy before it becomes entrenched, but it can be overcome at any point. To accomplish this, your daughter needs to understand how one form of envy, jealousy, takes root in the Crybaby Heart. There are five stages of jealousy according to authors Gregory L. White and Paul E. Mullen in their book *Jealousy: Theory, Research, and Clinical Strategies:*

1. **Suspecting the threat.** When your daughter is insecure or dependent on others, she is more likely to be jealous. In this stage, she interprets actions as warning signals that arouse her suspicion.

These thoughts may be either rational or irrational. For example, your daughter runs into her two best friends at the mall and immediately feels threatened. She suspects that her friends have purposefully excluded her. Her Crybaby Heart leaps at this signal and reinforces her insecurity.

2. **Assessing the threat.** This threat may be multiple, singular, or nonexistent. Sizing up the danger may involve the rational Courageous Heart or the irrational Crybaby Heart. When your daughter runs into her friends at the mall, she determines whether or not their trip to the mall together jeopardizes her relationship with them.

3. **Emotional reaction.** In this stage, jealousy can elicit a wide range of responses. The Crybaby Heart may feed jealousy with self-criticism, violent rage, embarrassment, or a sense of loss. The Courageous Heart may quiet jealousy with compassion, rational calm, confidence, or a sense of acceptance.

4. **Coping response.** Your daughter's coping response depends on whether she listens to her Crybaby Heart or her Courageous Heart. Outwardly, she may confront her friends directly with fairness or anger. Inwardly, she will make the choice to belittle or comfort herself by protecting or mending her damaged ego. Basically, she has two choices of outward and inward action depending on which aspect of her heart she listens to. If your daughter listens to her Crybaby Heart in the mall situation, then she might cope by writing off the friendship entirely or just wallowing in the "poor me" syndrome. If she listens to her Courageous Heart, she would quiet her jealousy with healthier responses. These responses may include realizing that going to the mall with her friends was not that important or she may just "tough it out" by controlling her jealousy.

5. **The outcome.** The bigger picture is what your daughter chooses to do with her emotion. This is her moment of choice. How she chooses to cope is her opportunity to triumph over envy or let envy defeat her. If your daughter lets her Crybaby Heart take control, the outcome is a proportionate loss of her self-esteem. If she lets her Courageous Heart take charge, she will triumph over envy and begin to heal her damaged ego.

Jealousy stems from a feeling that there is not enough to go around and that you will miss out. As a parent, you must remember that jealousy can arise when you compare your daughter with others. She is a unique individual. Praise her on her own merit, not based on others. Even when you compliment her, comparisons can be harmful. This leads her to make unfavorable comparisons. There will always be someone who is more talented, more skilled, or smarter than she is. This opens the door to envy and feelings of inadequacy. Comparing your daughter to others and not on her own merit shortchanges her.

Help your daughter realize that there is an abundance of things and that she is worthy of having them. Help her recognize when she is envious of someone or something and realize what has caused it. If she can pinpoint a specific event or a certain train of thought that triggered her jealousy, she can learn to react differently and break the thought pattern that caused the envy. Encourage your daughter to be thankful for what she does have. Her grateful heart can minimize her envy and multiply her gifts.

Insecurity and the pain of rejection are at the very root of envy. Understanding how envy can arise might help your daughter to identify and defuse it. Acknowledging envy can also take away some of its power. The best protection against envy is to empower the Courageous Heart to build a healthy self-image and believe in its ability to handle the green-eyed monster.

Deflective Blame

"It is a very common, ancient, well-perfected device for trying to feel better. Blame others. Blaming is a way to protect your heart, trying to protect what is soft and open and tender in yourself. Rather than own that pain, we scramble to find some comfortable ground."
— Pema Chodron, *In the Gap Between Right and Wrong*

An acceptable defense in trials today is to paint the perpetrator as the victim. A popular and acceptable defense for inappropriate actions is to blame the behavior on some outside force. A murderer blames his socially unacceptable actions on his deprived childhood. The jury sets him free. Society at large is blamed for the plethora of social ills in the world. Parents blame their children's friends for pulling them into drugs and crime. If their kids fail in school, they blame the teacher. Teens blame their peers for getting them into trouble. Personal accountability is almost nonexistent. In today's society, the blame game rules.

Mistakes and failings are part of the human condition and not always easy to acknowledge. It is a natural human trait to deny one's own role in creating these problems. People blame and criticize others because they dislike admitting wrongdoing, feeling guilty, and suffering the consequences. They blame others because the load of guilt is too heavy to bear. Blaming someone else is a convenient technique of the Crybaby Heart to keep a person from owning up to his or her own shortcomings. However, blaming someone else cannot protect anyone from the inevitable consequences. A person's wrongdoing will continue to be a fault until it is recognized and corrected.

Your daughter needs to realize that letting her Crybaby Heart blame someone else for a mistake is robbing her of the opportunity to explore and find a solution to the problem. Taking responsibility for the problem and the solution gives her power. By taking the responsibility, she allows herself the opportunity to explore solutions and regain control. Conversely, not taking the responsibility by blaming others takes away her power and makes her ineffective.

While she may not have control over the entire situation, she does have control over her response. Your daughter needs to know that everything she feels and everything she does comes from within her and not from someone or something else outside of her. How she chooses to think about what happens to her shapes her emotional well-being. When she blames others, she assumes a victim role. When she accepts responsibility, she grows. Phillip McGraw, Ph.D., in his book *Life Strategies: Doing What Works, Doing What Matters,* puts it succinctly, "You are accountable. Stop being a victim. . . . It's because you haven't created positive energy in your world. Go do it. You cannot blame other people."

Your daughter does not have to be harsh in blaming herself. Fairly accepting her culpability in the situation is all that is required of her. If she dwells on blaming others or herself, she wastes valuable time and energy that could be better spent. By taking an honest look at her own responsibility, she can learn from the experience and move forward.

Tips from the Toolbox

One of the best ways your daughter learns how to take personal responsibility is by watching how you handle accountability and blame. If you take responsibility when you are at fault, your daughter probably will, too.

- *Admit your mistake when it is your fault.*
- *Don't waste time blaming others.*
- *Avoid a victim mentality. Be assertive in taking control. Apologize when appropriate, and take the necessary steps to correct the situation.*
- *Help your daughter recognize the power she has in situations. She chooses how to respond.*

Paralyzing Fear

"'But how about my courage?' asked the Lion anxiously.
'You have plenty of courage. All you really need is some confidence in yourself,'
replied the Wizard. 'Every living thing is afraid when it faces danger.
True courage is facing danger even when you are afraid, and you already
have that kind of courage.'" — The Wizard of Oz by Frank Baum

What are you afraid of? Are you afraid of death or illness? Does making a decision scare you? Are you fearful of speaking in public? The fear of embarrassment, the fear of flying, the fear of rejection — whatever it is, you are not alone. Fear is a normal emotion. Healthy fear can prompt you to take action and help you to succeed. It is vital to your survival.

The Courageous Heart may use fear as an indicator. If your daughter fears a certain action, then the reasons for this fear must be examined. The presence of healthy fear may indicate the action is dangerous and should not be attempted. Fear may be a warning that someone may get hurt. For example, healthy fear may prevent your daughter from touching a hot stove or walking in front of a speeding car. In these cases, fear is a useful tool to enable your daughter to make a wise decision.

Another type of fear is foreign to the Courageous Heart. The Crybaby Heart uses paralyzing fear and anxiety to prevent your daughter from attempting new challenges. Fear redirects the focus of moving forward to an impotent feeling of "I can't." Underlying this fear is the fear that she won't be able to handle what life brings her. Your daughter's Crybaby Heart relishes this pessimistic "I can't" attitude and generates it to incapacitate and rule her life.

However, this fear can be overcome. If we realize that everybody feels fear when they do something outside of their comfort zone, yet some people accomplish a task despite their fear, then we can determine that fear is not the problem. The secret in handling fear is for the Courageous Heart to move from the Crybaby Heart's position of pain (helplessness, depression, and paralysis) to a position of power (choice, energy, and action).

 Tips from the Toolbox

Fear should be a guide. It should be used just like a car horn — to warn of danger. However, if the horn is sounded indiscriminately or gets stuck, its purpose is lost. As a warning, fear can be controlled and used by the Courageous Heart.

Have your daughter write down a few things that she fears. Are these fears warning of danger? If not, help her examine ways to overcome them.

Mismanaged Anger

"Anger is a stone cast into a wasp's nest" — Malabar Coast proverb

FIVE TRUTHS ABOUT FEAR

Susan Jeffers, Ph.D., reveals several profound truths about fear in her book *Feel the Fear and Do It Anyway*. These observations can help your daughter learn how to use her fear to motivate and accomplish, rather than paralyze.

1. The fear will never go away as long as I continue to grow.
2. The only way to get rid of the fear of doing something is to go out and do it.
3. The only way to feel better about myself is to go out and do it.
4. Not only am I going to experience fear whenever I'm on unfamiliar territory, but so is everyone else.
5. Pushing through fear is less frightening than living with the underlying fear that comes from a feeling of helplessness.

Anger is a powerful emotion. The Courageous Heart can use healthy anger to prompt your daughter to take social responsibility to right injustices such as racial or religious prejudices and stand up for fairness, truth, and moral goodness. Healthy anger also can be a personal response to protect your daughter from wrongs committed against her. At times, it is very appropriate to be angry. Martin Luther once remarked, "I never work better than when I am inspired by anger; for when I am angry, I can write, pray, and preach well, for then my whole temperament is quickened, my understanding sharpened, and all mundane vexations and temptations depart." Anger can be used to motivate to correct an injustice or an injury to the emotions. It is only when anger is mismanaged that it becomes problematic.

Experts have noted that mismanaged anger can be symptomatic

of underlying problems. Feelings of helplessness, low self-esteem, poor health, fatigue, and insecurity can all be underlying reasons for anger. Uncontrolled outbursts of anger and chronic anger have serious physical and psychological consequences. Anger can manifest itself in many ways: silence, jealousy, frustration, bullying, nagging, criticism, intolerance, insults, profanity, violence, abuse, vandalism, revenge, assault, murder, depression, and suicide. Mismanaged anger is costly and destructive to individuals as well as society.

Uncontrolled anger can sometimes splinter into passive-aggressive behavior. A preteen may use subtle resistance to display her anger. She may procrastinate, claim forgetfulness, or purposefully make herself inefficient. Roni Cohen-Sandler and Michelle Silver, in their book *I'm Not Mad, I Just Hate You! A New Understanding of Mother-Daughter Conflict*, accurately describe this form of anger. "Although superficially acquiescent, girls unconsciously may resist your demands and frustrate your authority, all while maintaining their good intentions. In this way, they are able to express hostility without taking any responsibility for it." The authors further note other common passive-aggressive behaviors that include forgetting to call you when they are late, subtly criticizing you to others, sabotaging your best-laid plans, and "accidents" such as ruining your clothes in the laundry or misplacing borrowed jewelry.

Consider this typical example of mismanaged anger. Suppose you ask your daughter to take out the trash. She agrees with no intention of fulfilling the request. When you remind your daughter later, she exhibits her displeasure by sullenly taking it as far as the back door. This behavior is passive-aggressive because while she does not outwardly resist or object, her hostility is revealed in her apathy. Her Crybaby Heart allows passive aggression to injure her in two ways. The empty promise to take out the trash depletes her integrity. Then, she is damaged again by a cowardly approach at displaying her anger. Passive-aggressive behavior damages others as well as herself. She damages herself with fear and dishonesty, while she causes others to distrust her.

Many young women are taught that it is not okay to feel or express anger. A girl's Crybaby Heart may tell her that her anger is not legitimate or that she has no right to be angry. This can cause her to bury her anger and discount her feelings. Repressed anger depletes the immune system and can cause sleep loss, increased heart rate, and stomach ulcers. Irritability, boredom, pessimism, depression, and mood disturbances are just a few of the conditions of pent-up anger. Repressed anger can build toward an emotional explosion and sometimes violence. Anger diminishes self-worth and optimism and increases stress and tension.

Health-care professionals advise people to determine what is and is not worth getting angry over, and to learn how to react in nonaggressive ways to situations that require attention. Your daughter's Courageous Heart can master skills to handle her anger and that of others. Learning to manage her anger helps your daughter resolve problems, not just react to them. To handle anger and not just react to it, your daughter must take ownership of her anger and the feelings it triggers in her. By learning to better communicate her feelings and by taking responsibility for them, she can view anger-producing situations as challenges to undertake.

Anger is a distorting emotion that your daughter's Crybaby Heart uses to narrow her life. To combat anger's destructive effects, she must determine what is and isn't worth getting angry about and then learn to express herself in an assertive manner. She can then allow her Courageous Heart to take responsibility for the anger and implement mechanisms to manage the emotion. Your daughter must learn to handle her own anger, as well as anger from others.

When your daughter's Crybaby Heart mismanages anger, she should first try to recognize her anger and where it is coming from. When she takes an honest look at her behavior, she might be able to reveal the source of her anger. Prayer, meditation, and relaxation techniques are often beneficial in diffusing anger, as well as paying attention to physical reactions and taking deep breaths. She should practice self-control and remain rational and calm. By following these hints, your daughter will be better equipped to defuse her own anger.

Perhaps even harder for your daughter to manage is anger from other people because she has control over her response but not theirs. However, her response is powerful because it can curtail or exacerbate another's anger. While everyone must tolerate some degree of anger, your daughter should develop skills to counteract any inappropriate or abusive anger directed toward her.

Inappropriate anger can empower your daughter's Crybaby Heart to control her emotions and alter her response. When your daughter is faced with inappropriate anger, she should initially evaluate whether the anger is justified. If she determines that the anger is inappropriate, she can try to establish a neutral common ground or refocus the conversation. If this fails, she should remove herself from the situation, if possible. These tools of the Courageous Heart are effective weapons to combat inappropriate anger.

Abusive anger is injurious behavior, whether it is physical or emotional. This anger berates, belittles, or diminishes another person's dignity. It is important not to tolerate abusive anger from others. If your daughter determines another person's anger is abusive, the first thing she should do is make her safety the priority. When things are calm, she may want to let the other person know that she will not tolerate the abuse. Your daughter should always make a conscious decision not to berate, belittle, or diminish another person's dignity, even if she is angry, nor should she allow this behavior from others. She should always remember that she has the right to be treated with dignity and respect, and she is not to blame for another person's abusive anger.

Inappropriate Guilt

"Guilt is the source of sorrows, the avenging fiend that follows us behind with whips and stings." — Nicholas Rowe

Guilt is an emotion that allows your daughter to examine whether her actions are in line with her values. Like anger and fear, guilt can be useful or inappropriate. As author Harlan J. Wechsler explains in *What's So Bad about Guilt?* there are two kinds of guilt. "On the one hand, guilt mirrors the mistakes that people make. When you feel guilty and it hurts, guilt is often precisely the right way to feel. On the other hand, many times when you feel guilty, it is precisely the wrong way to feel." First, let's examine the positive aspects of useful guilt.

The Courageous Heart can use the measuring stick of guilt to prompt your daughter to take responsibility for her actions. It is a calculated, measured emotion. The awareness of her guilt causes her discomfort. The Courageous Heart uses this conviction to adjust her actions and restore her comfort. By properly using this measuring stick to evaluate her actions, your daughter can assess her responses more accurately and fine-tune her decisions.

Guilt provides a measured response to transgression. How guilty your daughter feels should be proportionate to her behavior. Obviously, your daughter should not feel as much guilt if she were to get a speeding ticket as if she were to drive while under the influence of alcohol. A proportionate measure of guilt can feel uncomfortable enough to direct her decisions and behavior.

All people do not feel guilt. Guilt occurs only in those who adhere to a moral code. Guilt occurs only when your daughter violates her own standards or values, not those of other people. Her teachers, her coaches, and her peers may have standards for your daughter, but until she adopts these as her own, she will not feel guilty for violating them.

Guilt also occurs when she violates universal principles that have been incorporated into her heart. If your daughter accepts the Golden Rule as a basic truth in her life, she will support her belief by treating others as she would like to be treated. If she does not treat people fairly, she will feel pangs of guilt. The Courageous Heart uses guilt to allow her to align her behavior with her true values.

On the other hand, inappropriate guilt can wreak havoc in the Crybaby Heart. If given control, your daughter's Crybaby Heart may let others determine the degree of guilt she feels. For example, your daughter's friend might pressure her to join the tennis team. She knows she is entirely too busy, but she feels inappropriate guilt. Her Crybaby Heart reminds her that her friend joined the swim team at her request last year, and she really owes her. She allows her friend to convince her to join. This emotional manipulation is counterproductive and gives away her control.

When your daughter's Crybaby Heart calls for perfection, guilt is inappropriate. Perfection is impossible to achieve. Your daughter's expectations need to be realistic. Unnecessary guilt from feeling inadequate wastes time and energy because your daughter is striving for an unattainable goal. When she tries to be flawless, she is destined for failure. The Crybaby Heart's use of inappropriate guilt damages your daughter's confidence and her ability to act with courage.

Silencing the Crybaby Heart with Courage

"Courage is the ladder on which all the other virtues mount."
— Clare Boothe Luce

The Courageous Heart can overcome these damaging emotions with the positive emotions of happiness, gratitude, compassion, and forgiveness. By using these positive emotions to redirect her emotional focus, your daughter can generate the optimism necessary to implement the decisions she makes.

It is an ongoing challenge to quiet the Crybaby Heart. Your daughter's Crybaby Heart continually bewails that emotions happen to her and she has no control over them. It is up to her Courageous Heart to constantly squelch this erroneous notion. The decisions your daughter makes and their consequences depend in large part on whether she listens to her Courageous Heart. It takes a great deal of courage for her to move away from the Crybaby Heart's victim role and take responsibility for what happens in her life.

The misuse of the emotions of envy, blame, fear, anger, and guilt allows the Crybaby Heart to manipulate the decision-making process. Envy and

HOW TO RENDER INAPPROPRIATE GUILT POWERLESS

1. Acknowledge inappropriate guilt.
2. Forgive yourself for feeling inappropriate guilt.
3. Do not allow guilt to injure your self-esteem.
4. Use guilt as a learning experience to ensure better outcomes.

blame are the Crybaby Heart's best weapons in attacking your daughter's self-worth. There is no beneficial application for these enemies of the heart. They are worthless. By squandering the energy and time necessary for the Courageous Heart to resolve the conflict, they paralyze potential good.

Emotions are considered vital in moral training partly because having the right emotions leads to doing the right thing as a matter of course. When a sound decision is made, satisfaction, confidence, and happiness are some of the by-products that reinforce the decision. Joshua Halberstam states in his book *Everyday Ethics,* "Emotions are feelings aimed at a target." When the target is healthy decision making, the Courageous Heart evokes positive, appropriate emotions to support sound decisions.

It is the Courageous Heart's job to employ emotions to support appropriate decisions and redirect inappropriate decisions. While fear, anger, and guilt are often considered negative emotions, substantial benefits can be derived from each. The Courageous Heart must persevere to obtain the positive aspects of fear as an indicator, anger as a motivator, and guilt as a measuring stick to accurately direct actions. The Courageous Heart takes the best of these emotions to work for the heart, not against it. When the Courageous Heart successfully manages these emotions, the heart can more effectively interact with the other decision-making centers, the head and the gut, to generate sound decisions within the Connected Inner Guide.

The Courageous Heart must also guard against the negative emotions of envy and blame to successfully direct decisions. If your daughter wants to empower her Courageous Heart, she should always protect her heart against these emotions. Your daughter has the choice of redirecting or controlling hurtful emotions. This is the function of her Courageous Heart: to minimize and silence the Crybaby Heart's choking emotions of envy and blame.

Emotions can hurt and emotions can heal. The Courageous Heart uses the discomfort of fear, anger, and guilt to motivate your daughter to change. When this is honestly and carefully accomplished, the Crybaby Heart is silenced and the Courageous Heart can direct decisions accurately with happiness, compassion, and forgiveness. Happiness combined with forgiveness and compassion are the solutions to the misguided emotions of the Crybaby Heart. By incorporating these emotions into daily life, your daughter can learn to make wiser decisions and live with purpose and direction. Just like the negative emotions, happiness, forgiveness, and compassion are choices of the heart, and they must be chosen willfully. These emotions are vital for a healthy Courageous Heart, and more important, for your daughter's overall well-being.

Some emotions generally do not require a struggle in the Courageous Heart but can be extremely illusive. Everybody agrees on the importance of happiness and gratitude in a complete life. However, there is no simple recipe to obtain these emotions. The emotion of happiness is aimed at the core of a person's being. The pursuit of happiness is a worthwhile, ongoing endeavor of the Courageous Heart. Happiness and gratitude are emotions of the earnest heart.

The search for happiness is a driving force behind many actions, and next to good health, the foremost desire for many. Throughout time, when basic survival needs are met, people have searched for ways to achieve happiness. This endeavor is not a trivial matter. Our forefathers recognized its importance for a quality life. One of the self-evident truths in the Declaration of Independence is the inalienable right to the pursuit of happiness. In the modern high-tech world, a great amount of time and energy is devoted to this pursuit. The quest for happiness is the raison d'être for many of our daughters. In our world of instant gratification, people tend to define happiness by what makes them feel breathless and excited or thoroughly entertained and pampered. The pulse has to be racing and the adrenaline pumping, or the physical and mental senses packed with

> ## THE BEST THING IN THE WORLD
>
> "Brains are not the best thing in the world," said the Tin Woodsman.
>
> "Have you any?" inquired the Scarecrow.
>
> "No, my head is quite empty," answered the Tin Woodsman. "But once I had brains, and a heart also; so, having tried them both, I should much rather have a heart...for brains do not make one happy, and happiness is the best thing in the world."
>
> — *The Wizard of Oz* by Frank Baum

pleasure and enjoyment. Theodore Isaac Rubin states in Dennis Wholey's *Miracle of Change,* "It is hard to be happy in a society that confuses high stimulation with happiness."

Many of our daughters have not learned that the ability to be happy rests within, not in the false impression that outside stimulation is the source of happiness. They allow their Crybaby Heart to focus on obtaining happiness through outside events or people. This is foolhardy because other people cannot be held responsible for our daughters' personal happiness.

Our daughters must recognize that the instant gratification or stimulation overload of outside events will not achieve the elusive goal of happiness. The key to true happiness lies deep within. Our daughters should look inward to their Courageous Heart for the solution. This puts them in charge of their own inner happiness.

A large part of your daughter's life will be a trial-and-error search for the evasive goal of happiness. Life will be a roller coaster of ups and downs as long as the search is strictly for the stimulation or the "high." Your daughter's search for happiness through external sources is almost a guarantee that happiness will elude her. Life will moderate and feelings of happiness will occur when your daughter takes the responsibility and control for her own happiness. In fact, all she really has to do, according to Barry Neil Kaufman in his book *Happiness Is a Choice,* is decide to be happy. That is the one step in his program: Decide to be happy right now.

When your daughter's Courageous Heart makes the decision to be happy, an interesting thing happens. She finds that difficult decisions become clearer because she has a direction. These decisions are not as scary because she has the knowledge that no matter what happens, she will remain happy. Regardless of her circumstances, she chooses to be happy. Confidence and a sense of victory follow as she remains committed to being happy.

There is a cyclical quality to happiness and making sound decisions. Each has an impact on the other. Happiness is easier when your daughter makes sound decisions. And conversely, sound decisions are easier when your daughter is happy. Satisfaction, confidence, and peacefulness are some of the by-products that reinforce your daughter's sound decisions and lead to feelings of happiness. Then, a sense of empowerment follows to help your daughter make future sound decisions.

In the midst of difficult situations, your daughter will struggle to choose happiness. Parents can help by showing their daughters that happiness is an option, even during the most trying times. When your daughter chooses happiness, she automatically gains control and feels less helpless in what might have seemed an out-of-control situation.

One way your daughter can choose happiness is to learn the art of being grateful. Gratitude is at the core of true happiness. When your daughter incorporates a general attitude of gratitude into everyday thoughts, moments of happiness can be acknowledged and appreciated. Gratitude reminds her of all that she has been given. It tells her that although she may not have everything she wants, she probably has the things that she needs. The power of happiness combined with gratitude silences the negative feelings forced by the Crybaby Heart and allows the Courageous Heart to be the caretaker of the heart's emotions.

 Tips from the Toolbox

It is easy to be grateful when things are going well, but what about when times are bad? Viewing stressful situations as challenges or opportunities can be the cornerstone of a good self-image. Appreciating a tough situation can help expand your daughter's understanding, humility, and endurance. Challenges make her stronger. Help your daughter look to the positive and make it a habit to count her blessings.

Vicki, an eighteen-year-old freshman at University of Texas, realized her need to forgive when her long-time boyfriend, Michael, broke up with her and started dating another girl. She related, "I still love Michael so much, but I feel so betrayed. At times, I am so angry with him, and at others, I can't imagine my life without him. We even talked about marriage some day, but he just says it's over and wants to date other people. He's moved on and seems so happy. My heart hurts so much. Since I'm the one in pain, I know I'm the one who has to do something. I know I have to forgive, forget, and move on. It's just so hard." Vicki realized that her Crybaby Heart was allowing anger and blame to exacerbate her pain. It took a while, but six months after their breakup, Vicki was able to forgive Michael for the pain he had caused her. Once she chose to forgive Michael, she found that this was a turning point for her. Her Courageous Heart's forgiveness defused the anger and blame, allowing her to let go of the pain and move forward with her life.

Compassion and forgiveness infuse the heart and render powerless many of the painful emotions of the Crybaby Heart (blame, guilt, anger, and fear). The Courageous Heart employs compassion and forgiveness to release the hold of these enemies of the heart and silence them. Then, with time, compassion and forgiveness can heal the Crybaby Heart.

Compassion and forgiveness are acts of will. Your daughter can *choose* compassion or she *can choose* to be hard hearted. She either chooses to forgive or does not. However, in choosing to forgive, your daughter chooses to let go of the toxins of anger, fear, and blame that eat away her happiness and well-being. The Courageous Heart's efforts to consistently make the decision to forgive and be compassionate will diminish the negative effects of the Crybaby Heart.

Compassion is a learned skill that grows with practice. Dr. Matthew McKay and Patrick Fanning, in their book *Self-Esteem,* maintain that compassion can be enhanced by developing understanding, acceptance, and forgiveness.

1. **Understanding.** Your daughter must know what occurred and why. To understand the problem, she must learn the realities of the situation and the reasons behind it.

2. **Acceptance.** She must acknowledge the situation and the consequences that accompany it. This involves an acknowledgment of the facts, but not judgment.

3. **Forgiveness.** The third and most important component of compassion is the act of forgiving. This does not necessarily mean approval of the situation, but it does involve letting go of the past failures and mistakes and looking forward to the future. Compassion relies on the knowledge that she can build on the learning experience to ensure a better outcome in the future.

Compassion is a powerful tool of the Courageous Heart. By developing the components of understanding, acceptance, and forgiveness, your daughter can augment her compassion to strengthen her Courageous Heart and move forward.

One way your daughter can choose to be compassionate is to master the skill of forgiving. Forgiveness is at the core of compassion. Leo Buscaglia, Ph.D., in his bestseller *Loving Each Other,* states that "forgiveness is a freeing of self from the past and facing the future wiser, with renewed hope and faith." When a mistake is made, it is important to forgive. One of the best investments your daughter can make for her future is to forgive herself. Forgiveness allows her to wipe the slate clean, learn from her mistakes, and move forward.

No one is claiming forgiveness is easy. Buscaglia reminds us that there is nothing wrong with us if forgiveness comes hard. "We are simply human, vulnerable, and far from perfect. The wrong that people do us is difficult to deal with, especially when we are innocent and can find no explanation for another's behavior. Why should we forgive and forget? We forgive, for the price we pay for not forgiving is too great. To bear grudges, to harbor hate, to seek revenge, are all self-defeating and lead us nowhere. They neither satisfy nor heal. They keep us from moving forward and starting again. They bury positive energies in negative actions which serve only to exhaust and deplete us."

Your daughter must learn to forgive herself before she can forgive others. Forgiveness is a powerful coping skill to overcome feelings of anger, resentment, and revenge. Forgiving is setting a prisoner free and discovering that the prisoner was you. Many incorrectly view forgiveness as a gift to the person being forgiven. The real gift is to the person who forgives. By forgiving, your daughter is the beneficiary. Therapist and author Dr. Joan Borysenko, aptly terms forgiveness "freedomness," because it frees one from the cycle of hate and fear.

When your daughter forgives, she releases the disease-producing energy that produces hormones that poison her mental, emotional, and physical system. When she doesn't forgive, chemicals like adrenaline and cortisone are released. Not forgiving can cause high blood pressure, depression, ulcers, gastritis, and rage. In short, not forgiving can make her ill both physically and emotionally.

Forgiveness is not about excusing, denying, or hiding the event. The old adage "Forgive and forget" is probably not realistic. To forgive, your daughter must face reality and accept her anger. Forgiveness is about remembering the situation, recognizing what happened, letting go of the anger, and moving on. This is not easy and is often a slow, confusing process.

Your daughter can forgive and still have some anger. She can hold the person accountable. If the actions are repetitive, you can remind her that it might be desirable to step away from the offender's presence or sphere of influence. Even if she chooses to stay in the person's sphere of influence, she doesn't have to have the same relationship as before. She can learn from the situation and adjust her responses or learn to set appropriate boundaries to prevent further injury. (See "Boundaries: A Working Partnership" on page 15.)

When your daughter doesn't adjust her responses and continues to resent the person or situation, she gives them power over her. She cannot be happy if she is angry. Forgiving allows her to close doors from the past. Her forgiveness affirms that she is no longer controlled by what has happened. By taking charge of her life and letting go of the past, she gains strength.

If your daughter chooses not to forgive, she harbors toxins that might cause her to make unwise decisions. Your daughter's Crybaby Heart thrives in the affliction of unforgiveness. It wields undesirable emotions that cloud her reasoning and impair her judgment.

Forgiveness, on the other hand, is the Courageous Heart's armor of emotional and physical resilience. Your daughter's Courageous Heart can make more logical decisions when it is healthy. By forgiving and letting go of the pain associated with unforgiveness, her emotions don't get in the way of making competent decisions. Forgiving allows her Courageous Heart to support decisions that let go of the pain of unforgiveness and lead to her personal happiness.

 Tips from the Toolbox

Tell your daughter that her past is just that — past. She shouldn't let mistakes from her past have a negative hold on her future. Forgiveness and compassion can help her face her past and move forward. A good rule for putting the past into perspective is to use

the acronym P-A-S-T: Put Away. Start Today. Your daughter may want to remind herself of the acronym P-A-S-T and post it on her bathroom mirror or her bulletin board.

Ten Strategies to Overcome the Crybaby Heart

The following are some effective strategies to help your daughter redirect her Crybaby Heart's misguided emotions. Sometimes, a simple insight can be the catalyst that leads your daughter to a healthier emotional place. These strategies can help your daughter replace any negativity she has and move to the more constructive and motivating emotions of her Courageous Heart:

> ### FIVE STEPS TO FORGIVING
>
> 1. Understand what has hurt you.
> 2. Determine what you need to move on.
> 3. Communicate how you feel.
> 4. Make the decision to let go of the pain. (The time line is up to you.)
> 5. Continually work at maintaining the decision to let go.

1. **Avoid casting blame on any external force.** By taking personal responsibility for her thinking and her actions, your daughter gains control.

2. **Realize that the past can never be changed.** Any guilt, blame, or anger about the past will not change things. Getting stuck in guilt, anger, or blame can prevent your daughter from learning from her experience.

3. **Measure success by personal standards.** To guard against feelings of envy, your daughter should measure her success by her own standards, not those of others. There will always be someone who has more, does more, makes more. Allow her to be the best she can be and accept her as she is.

4. **Understand that gratitude is a choice.** The real art of gratitude is finding good in a bad situation. Become aware of any good that has resulted from a difficult situation.

5. **Realize that some fear is useful in pointing out dangers.** Everybody feels fear. However, fear should not paralyze. When your daughter realizes that she can handle anything that comes her way, fear loses much of its power. (See "Pragmatic Optimism" on page 136.)

6. **Choose to remove anger.** Your daughter can choose to eliminate anger from her life. While expressing anger is healthier than harboring it, not having anger at all is the healthiest choice.

7. **Take responsibility for personal happiness.** Because only she has control over her thoughts and actions, your daughter should take responsibility for her own happiness. Any external factors, people, or events can be bonuses to her happiness that enrich her life.

8. **Incorporate compassion to defuse anger, blame, and guilt.** Understanding, warmth, and flexibility are the keys to compassion and open the door to forgiveness.

9. **Learn to honestly forgive.** By forgiving, your daughter declares that she will not allow some event or person to control her any longer. Forgiving brings freedom to the forgiver.

10. **Discover and develop the Courageous Heart.** Happiness, gratitude, compassion, and forgiveness all thrive in a Courageous Heart.

FIFTEEN QUICK TIPS TO FEED YOUR COURAGEOUS HEART

1. Talk with a good friend.
2. Listen to uplifting music.
3. Pray.
4. Take a long walk.
5. Write in your journal.
6. Play a musical instrument.
7. Perform a small act of kindness.
8. Keep a promise.
9. Read an inspirational book.
10. Appreciate one new thing.
11. Sing out loud.
12. Take a hot bath.
13. Make a new friend.
14. Forgive an old hurt.
15. Have a good laugh.

Your daughter's heart can be transformed from the damaging Crybaby Heart to the grateful, forgiving Courageous Heart. This is an ongoing process of discovery and adjustment and does not happen overnight. As the Courageous Heart silences the Crybaby Heart, the heart becomes a powerful and welcome contributor to the decision-making process. When the Courageous Heart takes charge of your daughter's emotions, it can interact effectively with the head and the gut to generate sound decisions within her Connected Inner Guide. Next, let's take a look at the last component of the Connected Inner Guide, the gut, and explore its influence in our daughters' lives.

HONING THE SKILLS
What You Can Do

Understanding Your Daughter's Crybaby Heart — *This mental exercise will offer you a perspective on the challenges your daughter faces with her Crybaby Heart.*

How does your Courageous Heart handle your Crybaby Heart? What techniques do you use to quiet negative emotions? Recall how your Crybaby Heart reacted when you were a teen. Was your Courageous Heart as adept as it is now at handling your Crybaby Heart's challenges? How much of your Courageous Heart's strength is due to your level of experience and knowledge? Remember, your daughter does not have the benefit of experience to help to overcome her Crybaby Heart. How can you relate some of these experiences of growth in your own life to your daughter so she understands she is not alone?

Modeling Your Courageous Heart — *This activity is extremely important for your daughter to fully develop her own Courageous Heart.*

How you view the world and the emotions you use to react to situations have a tremendous impact on how your daughter chooses to view situations and react to them. When you allow your Crybaby Heart to overrule your rational emotions and make you feel you have no power in situations, your daughter is watching and learning. Discuss with your daughter recent situations in which you let your Crybaby Heart control your actions and how you corrected your mistake.

What You Can Do with Your Older Daughter (Ages Thirteen to Twenty-Three)

Overcoming Guilt — *This strategy will help reduce others' guilt manipulations.*

When others try to influence your daughter's actions by using guilt, teach her how to let others know their manipulation will not sway her. This exercise will also help her learn how to ask directly for her needs and not manipulate others with guilt. Play out roles where you use guilt and your daughter responds. Afterwards, play out the situation using appropriate responses.

- Pretend your daughter is not helping you cook Thanksgiving dinner. You play the martyr who is cooking the dinner all by yourself. You complain that your back hurts and there is too much to do, without ever asking your daughter to help. Your daughter should not let inflicted guilt influence her decision. Perhaps she could respond, "Mom, you're the one who is choosing to do all the work by yourself. If you need help, please ask." Once she defuses the guilt, the emotional manipulation is eliminated. Play the scene one more time where you ask her directly to help and she responds positively. Talk about how much better you both feel when guilt is not used and you use the appropriate emotional response.

- Pretend your college-age daughter has an opportunity to go skiing over spring break, but this means you will not see her until summer. You tell her that her cousin Ginny, whom she hasn't seen in several years, is coming to visit and she'll really disappoint Aunt Sophie if she isn't there. Talk about how you both feel at this point. Now replay the story by telling your daughter that Ginny will be visiting, but you understand her dilemma. Be honest that you will miss seeing her, but whatever she chooses, be supportive. Again, discuss how you feel when guilt is not a factor in making decisions.

Learning to Forgive — *This activity will remind you and your daughter of the importance of forgiveness and compassion.*

Refer to "The Five Steps to Forgiving" found on page 85. Have your daughter think about something someone has done that has hurt her. She may prefer to do this privately. Now, discuss with her the five steps to forgiving. Make it clear that forgiving benefits the forgiver. This does not necessarily mean she must forget about the incident, but she does need to release its hold on her.

Overcoming the Crybaby Heart — *This exercise will help you and your daughter see how to change your emotions and redirect them.*

Join your daughter in sitting down and thinking of a difficult situation that you each might face. Be aware of all the options you both have. Next, you and she should close your eyes and picture feeling happy about it, feeling angry about it, forgiving, blaming, feeling fearful and courageous, and so on. Write down all the possible feelings about the situation. This will help both of you see that you have a choice in how you feel and react.

What You Can Do with Your Younger Daughter (Ages Six to Twelve)

Overcoming Blame — *This game is helpful in teaching your daughter some alternatives to blame and anger.*

Use these scenarios to discuss with your daughter that blaming and complaining will not solve the situation and that she can choose not to blame or hold on to anger.

- Your daughter's friend is always at least a half hour later than she says she will be. Have your daughter think of five ways she can react differently, instead of blaming and complaining about her friend. For example, she can use the time to do something else while she waits, or she can tell the friend to call if she is running late, et cetera.
- Your daughter's teacher gives her a poor grade on a project that she worked hard on. Try to think of at least three ways your daughter can react that avoids blame. For example, she might discuss with the teacher what she missed and how she could improve.

■ Your daughter shares a room with her younger sister. She blames her sister for the mess and uses this as an excuse not to keep the room neat. Discuss ways she can take responsibility for her room. Perhaps she could set aside a time once a day when she and her sister could work together to straighten the room.

Understanding True Happiness — *This activity can help your daughter become aware of the many nonmaterial sources of happiness.*

Sit down with your daughter and each list as many things as you can that make you happy. Then, check all the ones that do not involve a material item. Share your lists with each other. If her list has more material possessions, help her think about other things that can make her happy, such as her grandmother's hugs or her puppy greeting her at the door.

Chapter Four

FROM CREEP TO TRAINED CONSCIENCE
The Gut's Role in Making Decisions

"If you would but listen and heed this wiser voice within, it will point you in the right direction. Use it as your compass to navigate from your port of entry to your final destination, to steer your ship along the journey of life in the safest, surest, most meaningful way possible." — Plato

As the master tool of decision making, the Connected Inner Guide gives our daughters an integrated three-part method to making choices and accepting responsibility. This chapter takes a look at the third center of decision making in the Connected Inner Guide, the gut. As with the other components of the Connected Inner Guide, there is a dual nature to the gut. These two facets are the Trained Conscience and the Creep. However, because the Creep is basically a void — a lack of values and principles — we'll focus primarily on the Trained Conscience and how it works as the vehicle of decision making within the gut.

Within the Connected Inner Guide, the gut incorporates personal values and universal principles to define what is and is not acceptable. These personal values and universal truths, when violated in a healthy Connected Inner Guide, stir discomfort or uneasiness within the gut. Your daughter's gut reaction indicates that she has a place at the core of her being that is at peace or disturbed depending on how she follows its truths. The gut is the deep-seated habitat for your daughter's values and principles.

Everyone has a personal value system. At one extreme of this value system lies the Creep whose purpose and direction are exclusively amoral. These are the Charles Mansons and the Ted Bundys of the world. At the other end of this spectrum lies the Trained Conscience whose sole purpose is moral excellence. These are the Mother Teresas in the world. However, most people fall somewhere along this spectrum.

Incorporating values is a life skill, and as a skill, it can be taught. No matter where your daughter is in her moral development, how old she is, or even what outside influences affect her, her value system can be improved. Family, peer groups, the media, early schooling, and some believe, even genetic makeup all influence your daughter's moral development, according to Joshua Halberstam in *Everyday Ethics*. Any of these influences can become your daughter's teacher. Halberstam further states, "The way we teach our children values goes a long way toward determining their later moral character.... And, as with so many other subjects, there is no better way to teach morality than by example."

Everything you do shows your daughter your value system. As journalist Jane Pauley observes, "Kids learn more from example than from anything you say. I am convinced they learn very early not to hear anything you say, but watch what you do." Although you may be telling your daughter how to live a moral life, your actions are speaking louder than your words. Your role in shaping her moral character should not be underestimated.

Your daughter's moral character is important because it influences the quality of decisions she makes. Her values shape her ability to make competent decisions. As universal principles are adopted by her Trained Conscience, they become the foundation for her personal set of values. In the decision-making process, her Trained Conscience incorporates universal principles and personal values to arrive at the best possible alternatives.

Several universal principles are often incorporated into a person's value system. While the following list is far from complete, it details many principles that are most valuable to a healthy Connected Inner Guide.

Universal Principles: Building Standards

"There is a law that man should love his neighbor as himself. In a few hundred years it should be as natural to mankind as breathing or the upright gait; but if he does not learn it he must perish." — Alfred Adler

Although your daughter's values are uniquely hers, they are tied to universal principles that are found in all people throughout history. True wisdom spans the ages. Throughout secular and religious literature, there is an acceptance that certain truths of collective wisdom exist. Some refer to these recurring themes as universal or natural laws; others call them true north principles or the inner compass. Much can be learned by studying these universal principles. They are the building standards for constructing a successful and rewarding life. Some of the universal principles that the Trained Conscience may incorporate into personal values include

- Basic Needs: The Upward Path
- Cause and Effect: The Consequence of Choice
- Experience: A Valuable Teacher
- The Golden Rule: The Relationship Adage
- Life: More than "Me" and "Now"
- Reaping What You Sow: Getting Back What You Give
- Harmony and Balance: Living in Tune with Nature
- Moderation: Wisdom's Companion
- Faith: Belief in a Higher Being

These universal principles, when incorporated by the Trained Conscience into a healthy Connected Inner Guide, yield an awareness of life and the depth of its connectedness. The first universal principle illustrates that certain needs must be met to grow.

Basic Needs: The Upward Path

According to humanistic psychologist Abraham Maslow, higher motives appear only after the more basic needs have been satisfied. For instance, if you are starving, you probably do not care what people think of your table manners. Your basic need for food is the strongest and must be met first. The basic human needs of food, shelter, and safety are at the bottom of Maslow's hierarchy of needs. As these needs are met, you can address higher needs until you reach the top of the hierarchy, self-actualization. Maslow describes this process of self-actualization as an attempt to become all that you can possibly become. He describes people who are self-actualized as people who listen to their own voices, take responsibility, are honest, and work hard. Self-actualized people appear to have, or to have had, peak experiences of insight, joy, or intense awareness. Becoming a self-actualized person is an underlying desire of your daughter's healthy Connected Inner Guide.

As discussed in chapter 1, your responsibility as a parent is to provide a safe, secure environment with unconditional love. When you satisfy your daughter's basic needs, your daughter can move up the hierarchy of needs to reach her true potential.

Cause and Effect: The Consequence of Choice

In nature, Isaac Newton's third law of motion states for every action there is an equal and opposite reaction. This is manifest throughout life. All actions have consequences associated with them. Actions or behaviors are the result of the choices your daughter makes. Good decisions at the moment of choice usually ensure better consequences. Author Ben Aaronvitch, contributing writer of the *Dr. Who* series, emphasizes the cause-and-effect relationship of decisions. "Every great decision creates ripples — like a huge boulder dropped in a lake. The ripples merge, rebound off the banks in unforeseeable ways. The heavier the decision, the larger the waves, the more uncertain the consequences."

You can help your daughter understand the cause-and-effect relationship of decision making by teaching her that her actions do have consequences.

There is an old expression, "You're getting what you're getting because you're doing what you're doing. If you don't like what you're getting, change what you're doing." Life is better for your daughter to the extent that she realizes her choices do have consequences and that she aligns her actions with the universal truths or the intuitive right thing to do.

Experience: A Valuable Teacher

Experience, whether good or bad, is a valuable teacher. Learning what works enables your daughter to duplicate her actions to achieve the desired results. Conversely, learning what doesn't work allows her to adjust her behaviors accordingly. Her experiences give her the groundwork for her Connected Inner Guide to improve her decision-making skills.

Mistakes are the prerequisite for the learning process. Your daughter cannot learn without making errors. A process that describes this principle is called "successful approximation." Successful approximation refers to the act of getting closer and closer to successful performance through the feedback provided by mistakes. The first time your daughter tried to walk, she fell. However, through many attempts, she learned to walk. By correcting her mistakes and continuing to try, she learned.

Aldous Huxley, who wrote *Brave New World,* notes, "Experience is not what happens to a man. It is what a man does with what happens to him." You can help your daughter learn the value of experience by showing her that mistakes are a necessary part of her growth. As your daughter grows, her experience will be a valuable tool in helping her obtain the wisdom she needs to make competent decisions.

The Golden Rule: The Relationship Adage

Most people are familiar with the Golden Rule, "Do unto others as you would have them do unto you." The Bible, the Koran, and the Torah all issue this edict. This law of human interaction is invaluable in lending your daughter compassion, appreciation, and insight in relating to others.

An interesting truth associated with this universal principle is that the way your daughter treats others always reflects the way she thinks of herself. In *Everyday Ethics,* Joshua Halberstam observes that this correlation between self-image and behavior exists in all people. When your daughter feels bad about herself, she is less likely to have a generous spirit in dealing with others. Your daughter's understanding of her own innate worth is an integral component to putting this universal principle into practice.

Life: More than "Me" and "Now"

Teenagers are notorious for living for themselves and failing to think beyond the immediate moment. As teens mature, they begin to realize the universal principle that life is far more intricate than "me" and "now." Everywhere you look, you can see examples of this principle. The news is filled with headlines and stories that will impact the future in some way. Natural disasters, cloning, technological strides, new political leaders, and medical breakthroughs all will shape the years to come. Events build on other events and may alter the course of life many times. Life is more complex than the present moment and more complicated than the individual.

When your daughter looks at the bigger picture and considers the impact of her actions, she makes better decisions. Within her Connected Inner Guide, her Trained Conscience is better equipped to handle tough decisions when she goes beyond the "me" and the "now."

Reaping What You Sow: Getting Back What You Give

Many religions incorporate the philosophy that the more you give, the more you get. The Eastern spiritual law of karma teaches that the good you do will come back to you, and conversely so will the evil. Western philosophy states that you reap what you sow. It is a universal truth that you get back what you give.

Your daughter's awareness of this universal principle can guide her in a positive direction. Nineteenth-century Russian scholar George Ivanovitch Gurdjieff describes this universal truth: "If you help others, you will be helped, perhaps tomorrow, perhaps in one hundred years, but you will be helped. Nature must pay off the debt.... It is a mathematical law and all life is mathematics." If your daughter sows good seeds, this good will be returned to her.

Harmony and Balance: Living in Tune with Nature

There is an old African saying, "When elephants fight, it is the grass that suffers." Living in tune with nature is a tenet found in many faiths. In Buddhism, the first commandment is a respect for life. In Yiddish, the toast *L'Chaim* is a salute to life. In Christianity, not even a sparrow falls without the Creator knowing. These beliefs emphasize the long-term effects of our actions and the reverence for life itself. At the core of existence is a life dependent on nature, which must be revered and protected. This universal principle requires an environmental stewardship or responsibility for the whole.

The importance of the earth and its relationship to life can best be summarized by the Great Law of the Haudenosaunee, Iroquois Six Nations, which states, "In all our deliberations we must take into account the well-being of the seventh generation to follow us."

Moderation: Wisdom's Companion

As children, many of us recall adults often saying, "Moderation in all things." When said, others murmured in agreement, sagely nodding their heads. Obviously they believed this was good advice. They understood that extremes complicate the equation of a balanced life.

When your daughter's Trained Conscience adopts the principle of moderation, her balanced perspective yields wisdom in the decision-making process. Moderation may mean the difference in whether or not she finishes the race, sustains herself during tough times, and appreciates the ebb and flow of life.

Our society of excesses often maligns the basic principle of moderation, saying that moderation means suppression or repression, that it is cowardly, not passionate, or simply, that it is dull. However, the test of time has proven the validity of the universal principle of moderation. Great minds such as Aristotle and Ben Franklin have recommended moderation in all things.

Faith: Belief in a Higher Being

Rabbi Joseph Telushkin, author of *Jewish Literacy*, defines faith as "complete confidence and belief in something we cannot see or prove. Throughout history, man has believed in a Supreme Power or Being who has not only created the world and humankind, but who cares about us individually and collectively." Faith in a Higher Being provides man with peace, unconditional love, joy, hope, healing, acceptance, forgiveness, awareness, freedom from fear, and abounding miracles.

As your daughter grows in her faith, she strengthens her decision-making skills by validating the truths of her Trained Conscience. Practicing her faith gives her guidance in making decisions. Her faith in a Higher Being then grounds her decisions with a sense of purpose and direction.

Faith in a Higher Being is a valuable resource for your daughter. A foundation in faith takes away a "self" focus and connects her with all humanity. It links her to all time, space, and existence. This relationship ties her to those who have gone before, and obligates her to those who will follow.

The gut's healthy Trained Conscience relies on these universal principles to provide a foundation for its personal value system. Although there are no set formulas for living, these universal principles provide guidance and clarity. Sean Covey, author of *The Seven Habits of Highly Effective Teens*, states, "Principles will never fail you. They will never talk behind your back. They don't get up and move. They don't suffer career-ending injuries. They don't play favorites based on skin color, gender, wealth, or body features. A principle-centered life is simply the most stable, immovable, unshakable foundation you can build upon, and we all need one of those."

Abiding by these universal principles allows your daughter to nurture and reinforce her personal values. Her Trained Conscience can thrive when her personal values are in line with adopted universal principles.

Personal Values: The Instruction Manual

"Try not to become a man of success but rather try to become a man of values."
— Albert Einstein

Common threads found in philosophy unite a people in a system of values. Values as defined in sociology are the acts, customs, and traits regarded in a favorable way by a people. Throughout history, societies have found different traits worthwhile. In *Self-Esteem*, Dr. Matthew McKay and Patrick Fanning compare a few of the characteristics that different cultures value. The Greeks as a society valued personal virtue as it contributed to the society's order; the Romans, patriotism and valor; the Christians, the love of God and mankind; the Buddhists, the removal of worldly desires; the Hindus, the reverence for all living beings; and the Muslims, law, tradition, and order.

Today, some Americans have developed a distorted value system. As an example, many adults value the job. You *are* what you do. When you meet someone, often the first question asked after you are introduced is "What do you do?" Your career often defines who you are to others. This emphasis on the job may ensure your economic success, but does it ensure a healthy, emotionally stable individual? Does it lead to happiness? What occurs if you become unemployed? This emphasis on what a person does for a living as their source of value does not adequately reflect their worth at all.

Because many Americans share this distorted view on the value of an individual, where can your daughter find her true worth? What others esteem as desirable matters less when your daughter develops and relies on her own set of personal values. Her personal values are deeper than the traits society views as important. They are what really and honestly matter to her. As her personal value system develops and grows, her decisions can rely on her personal values and not that of society.

Personal values are integral factors in making decisions. What your daughter does and does not value will be the basis for her actions. If your daughter values honesty, her decisions will incorporate truth. If she esteems patience, she will act with restraint. If your daughter does not value perseverance, she may give up easily. If she does not value hard work, she may not be willing to do the studying necessary to get an A. Personal values, whether good or bad, will affect the choices she makes.

Seventeen-year-old Nicole, a Midwestern senior at a private school, demonstrates how her personal value of honesty influenced an important decision. Nicole knew she needed at least a 3.5 GPA to get into the college of her choice. She was struggling in her pre-calculus class and really needed to make an A on the final exam to maintain her GPA. However, when her friend Amanda offered to give her a copy of the final test, Nicole refused, knowing that her refusal meant added work and uncertainty for her. Because her Trained Conscience embraced honesty, maintaining her integrity superseded her temptation to cheat. Nicole's reliance on her healthy Trained Conscience prevented her from betraying her personal value system.

Decisions are influenced by accompanying underlying motives. Honesty was at the crux of this motivation for Nicole. Nicole realized that the means to obtain the grade mattered enough not to violate her value system. Honesty is an intrinsic good. In examining personal values, you should note the distinction between *instrumental goods* and *intrinsic goods*. Simply put, this involves understanding the difference between the means and the ends. An intrinsic good is something that has value in itself. Honesty is an intrinsic good because it has value. An instrumental good is something that leads to the intrinsic good, or is instrumental in attaining the intrinsic good. Had Nicole focused on the instrumental good of the grade itself, she might have jeopardized her intrinsic good of honesty. In today's quest for instant gratification, instrumental goods often become the focus, instead of the more lasting intrinsic goods.

Happiness is another example of an intrinsic good. Today, in alarming numbers, people view possessions as the source of happiness. They erroneously view instrumental goods like material possessions as intrinsic goods.

Some people spend a great deal of time and effort pursuing the dollar, fame, and power, and too little time enjoying the intrinsic goods that these are supposed to provide.

Many people confuse the means with the ends and put life's intrinsic goods on hold while pursuing the means. The way they spend their time and effort does not reflect their stated goals and values. They espouse goals of happiness and a life of honesty and integrity, but the message in their actions is very different: They reveal a drive for material possessions, but little else. To your teenager, who studies adults in an effort to learn, this is confusing.

It is understandable, then, that many teens view possessions as a desirable goal. It is not unusual for a teen to confuse getting a new car or making a certain athletic team as happiness. This view is distorted because the new car or the team in itself will not bring happiness. The new car could allow her the opportunity to spend more time with her friends, deepening friendships. The car then can be instrumental in leading to the happiness of friendship, but the car is not happiness. The desired athletic team may allow her to develop new skill levels, make new friends, and improve her fitness. The team is not the reason for happiness but may be the instrument to increase her happiness. When your daughter follows her value system and does not hold possessions or achievements as a goal, she gains direction and insight.

Values are your daughter's instruction manual to follow in taking responsibility and control in her life. Joshua Halberstam in *Everyday Ethics* shows how values, responsibility, and control interrelate. He states, "In the domain of your values, you reign supreme — no one else decides your values for you. To the extent that you're in control of your values, you're in control of your life."

Halberstam goes on, "Some people walk into a party and you know immediately that you can't mess with their self-definition. You may like them or not, but they are what they are. What does the self-defined person have that others lack? It's not charm, social skill, or confidence. It is self-respect. The self-defined individual has and knows she has, a solid core of values. . . . Because your values depend, finally, on you and no one else, you are more responsible for them than any of your other characteristics."

Tips from the Toolbox

Help your daughter determine what her intrinsic values are. To do this, she should evaluate what is important. What does she truly value? What does she need to be happy?

Often, extreme circumstances point to values. An interesting exercise to pinpoint what matters in your daughter's life is to pretend the world and all of mankind will end in ten days. How would she spend this time? What would she do and with whom? The choices she makes probably exhibit her current values. As she grows in maturity and wisdom, her values may change.

The Trained Conscience uses values as the compass to direct your daughter throughout her life. Using values to determine the next move, to make the next decision, to foresee the likely consequences, is simply practical. To relinquish control to the pulse-racing, adrenaline-pumping whim or the pampered, entertained selfish moment is to lose control of the tool that guarantees the path to a life interspersed with happiness. Letting outside stimulation or people control personal values, even for a short time, leads to destructive behaviors and a loss of self-esteem.

The merit of personal values and sometimes the very existence of these values are best shown when they are tested. When values are tested, the talk must be walked for the value to be real. Values that survive testing hold true. Without temptation, values are merely statements — empty, passive wishes too lofty to attain.

Although life may not always be fair or logical, a predetermined set of personal values may be the rock that anchors your daughter through rough times. In his bestseller *First Things First,* Stephen Covey notes, "People who listen to and live by their conscience do not have the cotton-candy satisfaction of urgency addiction, pleasing other people, or getting their security from being incredibly busy every minute. [The people who listen to their Trained Conscience] experience deep fulfillment. They are strong in hard moments. They have a high balance in their personal integrity account."

Covey describes this personal integrity account as the amount of trust we have in ourselves, in our ability to walk our talk. Your daughter's personal integrity account can grow by adhering to the unique values and principles that her Trained Conscience uses to guide her actions. Every time she follows her value system, the account grows and the Trained Conscience increases in strength. Confidence grows as the account grows.

By building her personal integrity account, your daughter's personal failures and negative behaviors are not as devastating. Small withdrawals are okay because there is a substantial account balance to solve the problems. Her reserves in her integrity account prevent her from faltering due to an occasional wrongdoing and allow her to have faith in her ability to make decisions.

Your daughter needs to understand that just doing the small things that she says she will do builds her personal integrity account. If she says she will wash the dog after school and she follows through with her promise, this adds to her account. She has done what she said she would do. Conversely, every time she says, "I'll wash the dog," and doesn't, every time she lies even about small matters, a piece of her personal integrity account is withdrawn.

If the integrity account balance is constantly being withdrawn, the negative component of the gut, the Creep, emerges. The Creep depletes the account balance along with feelings of self-worth. If allowed to rule, the Creep bankrupts the gut of values and principles. The Creep is just as worthless as the integrity account it empties.

Your daughter should be aware that the Creep is not always obvious in its maneuvers to destroy. The conniving Creep can slowly deplete your daughter's personal integrity account to the point that she does not notice its withdrawals. The Creep as a decision-making center

PERSUASIVE PHRASES OF THE CREEP

- Try it. You'll feel good.
- Just once won't hurt.
- You're mature enough to do this. Go for it.
- Everybody else does. Why not?
- Don't you want to be popular?
- It will help you get what you want, pass the test, get a date, make the team, et cetera.
- Nobody will know.

invalidates the heart and corrupts the head with its subtle thievery. However, the Trained Conscience can defeat the corruption of the Creep with a wall of honor built one brick at a time with personal and universal values (see page 219). Your daughter must decide for herself how much she will let the Trained Conscience or the Creep control her decisions.

Ten Strategies to Overcome the Creep

Values can be altered and enhanced through training and practice. Recognizing and defeating the tactics of the Creep require a commitment to augment and strengthen the Trained Conscience. Here are some strategies that can aid your daughter in developing her Trained Conscience:

1. **Devise a plan of action.** Your daughter should rehearse appropriate reactions and thoughts to use in enticing situations. When your daughter plans her reactions, she is better prepared to stand up for her values in a dangerous situation.

2. **Build personal values on adopted universal principles.** By building on a foundation of proven universal principles, your daughter establishes the groundwork for good decisions.

3. **Prioritize long-term consequences over short-term gratification.** There can be long-term negative consequences when your daughter makes immediate self-gratification the goal.

4. **Make a positive impact on the environment.** Your daughter can live more mindfully when she respects and takes care of her environment.

5. **Keep the Golden Rule.** Your daughter can avoid much pain and injury when she remembers others basically need to be treated the same as she would like to be treated.

6. **Be truthful.** When your daughter means what she says and says what she means, she builds her personal integrity account.

7. **Live purposefully.** Your daughter should make goals that are clear,

reachable, and reasonable. This will give her direction and help her to gain confidence.

8. **Follow up beliefs with actions that support them.** If your daughter values generosity, she should be generous. If she values hard work, she should work hard. Actions that support values reinforce them.

9. **Practice faith.** Your daughter's faith in a Higher Being will guide her in establishing and acting true to her values.

10. **Discover and develop the Trained Conscience.** When your daughter acts according to her values and principles, her Trained Conscience can be a powerful influence within the Connected Inner Guide.

The Trained Conscience guides actions and thoughts, and aligns them with values and principles. When the Trained Conscience speaks, self-awareness and a sense of personal integrity increase. Teach your daughter to listen to her Trained Conscience. It provides clues to the right or wrong of the situation. It is a gift to preserve the soul.

THE FROG IN THE POT

Warning: The Creep can slowly deplete the values in the Trained Conscience, bankrupting your daughter before she knows it.

There is an old tale that tells of two frogs. One frog was dropped into a pot of hot water. Feeling the intense heat, she jumped out and saved her life. Another frog was not so lucky. This frog was put into a pot of cold water — set on a burner over low heat. The temperature was increased one degree at a time. The frog became accustomed to it, stayed in the pot, and was boiled to death.

The moral: Although your daughter may be uncomfortable with a sudden change of values, it's often the gradual, hardly perceptible alterations in her values that can destroy her.

Your daughter's personal values must agree with the foundation on which they were built (her adopted universal principles) for her value structure to be stable and support sound decisions. When she makes her values and principles a priority, the Connected Inner Guide's Trained Conscience contributes moral soundness and decency to her decisions.

Good decisions accumulated over time build self-worth and increase confidence. The hammer of decision making, the Connected Inner Guide, shapes your daughter's choices with a balanced and integrated head, heart, and gut approach. Because the Connected Inner Guide is the control center responsible for decision making, ultimately it controls the quality of her life. In the next chapter, you will see how this integrated tool, the Connected Inner Guide, truly becomes the hammer of decision making.

HONING THE SKILLS
What You Can Do

Prioritizing Your Family's Activities — *This exercise offers you a perspective on prioritizing actions.*

Is your family life balanced? Are you too busy? Too much of anything, even good things, can cause stress, fatigue, and anxiety. Are you placing too much emphasis on one aspect of your daughter's life? Does she feel pressured? Make the choice to keep your family life balanced and in perspective.

Modeling Your Values — *This ongoing activity helps you align your actions with your value system.*

For the next week, spend time each evening reviewing your day. How have you conducted yourself in your daily routine? Perhaps you were impatient or rude while you waited in line at the store. Maybe you cut off other cars to enter the expressway. Did you tell a "white lie" and ask your daughter to say you weren't home when a salesperson called? If you value honesty, courtesy, and patience then your actions might not be reflecting your values. As you continue through the week, try to better model your values.

What You Can Do with Your Older Daughter (Ages Thirteen to Twenty-Three)

Learning from Your Experiences —*This exercise helps your daughter see how past endeavors can be learning tools.*

Look back at page 97 on experience as a valuable teacher. List some successful approximations you and your daughter have experienced in each of your lives. Some examples might be piano playing, swimming, soccer, spelling, painting, or sewing. Was there ever any activity you did perfectly the first time? Probably not. Now, discuss with your daughter a difficult project you are each working on. Every time you modify your approach with the knowledge you gain from your experience, you come closer to success.

Ranking Your Trained Conscience — *Your daughter may find this quiz helpful and fun in determining whether her actions are in line with her values.*

1. Your friend tells you her brother has access to some stolen merchandise and she can get you a $100 CD player for $10. She asks if you are interested. You respond
   A. Yes, I love a bargain.
   B. I love a bargain, but it is stolen. No.
   C. No. (And you tell your parents.)
   D. No. How dare you involve me?

2. Think about the names you hate to be called. You use these names to describe others
   A. A lot.
   B. Sometimes, but not to their face.
   C. Rarely or never. I understand how hurtful it can be.
   D. Occasionally. After all, some people are really stupid.

3. An acquaintance you would like to become friends with tells you an offensive joke. You
   A. Think it's funny and tell others.
   B. Laugh. You would really like to become friends.
   C. Don't laugh, and ask the person not to tell that type of joke to you.
   D. Exclaim in a bold voice how wrong it is, and consequently, you would never be her friend.

4. The clerk at the store miscounts and gives you $10 extra in your change. You

A. Keep it. It's not your fault that he miscounted.

B. Keep it but drop $5 in the charity box at the front of the store.

C. Tell the clerk and give it back.

D. Tell the clerk how stupid she is.

5. Your friend tells you she is going to try the latest trendy drug. You both know people who have tried it and loved it. However, you have heard about serious problems with it. You

A. Ask her to describe its effects to you. Once probably won't hurt her.

B. Keep your mouth shut. It's her business.

C. Try to dissuade her.

D. Tell her she's a loser, and this kind of behavior is just what you would expect of her.

6. You have made a promise not to ride with anyone who is drinking. After a party, you need a ride home. Your friend's brother arrives to take you and his sister home. He has obviously been drinking. You

A. Jump in the car and hope for the best.

B. Get a ride from a neighbor who is picking up her daughter, and say nothing.

C. You decline the ride and call your parents.

D. Find another ride, and figure if he has a wreck, it is his own fault.

7. Your friend has told you a secret and sworn you to secrecy. You

A. Tell your group. They would want to know.

B. Tell your best friend. She can keep her mouth shut.

C. Don't tell anyone even though it is tempting, unless it involves her health or safety.

D. Think to yourself, "Who cares?" and forget that you were supposed to keep quiet.

8. Your best friend is going out with a loser. You

A. Ask her if he has any friends. Then you could all hang out together.

B. Keep your mouth shut. It is her life.

C. Tell her you don't agree with her choice, but you value her friendship.

D. Dump her. After all, her judgment is poor.

9. You have a curfew. The rest of your group can stay at the party one hour later. You

A. Ignore the curfew and come in as late as you want. After all, you are going to be punished anyway.

B. Drive home too fast, trying to get in before the curfew, because you don't allow enough time.

C. Call home and ask for an extension of the curfew. Your parents would worry if you arrived late.

D. Make it home by your curfew, but tell your friends they have to find their own way home, because you want to enjoy every minute of the party.

Scoring

If you answered mostly A's, the Creep is controlling too many of your decisions. It appears you are only interested in short-term satisfaction and rarely consider the consequences of your actions. You probably need to seriously reevaluate your value system.

If you answered mostly B's, your Trained Conscience is trying to take control of your decisions, but there is room for improvement. You are moving in the right direction if you continue to look to your Trained Conscience and base your decisions on your values and principles.

If you answered mostly C's, you consider the long-range consequences as well as your values in making decisions. Congratulations! You are in tune with your Trained Conscience and are well on your way to a life of integrity.

If you answered mostly D's, you know what you stand for, but others may find you too judgmental and overbearing. Try to temper your Trained Conscience by treating others with a little more understanding and consideration.

What You Can Do with Your Younger Daughter (Ages Six to Twelve)

Determining Others' Values — *This activity helps your daughter see how actions reveal values.*

> Pick a movie you and your daughter have seen recently to review together. What were some of the choices the main characters made? What did their actions say about their values? Ask your daughter what she would have done differently if she were the main character? How would her values affect her choices? Would the outcome be the same?

Realizing the Future Depends on Today — *This dialogue helps your daughter incorporate the universal principle of cause and effect: the consequence of choice.*

> Take today's newspaper and look at it with your daughter. Do you see any events that can change the future? Talk about what events you think might follow. Name some people who might help in the situation. Can you think of something you could do to help the outcome?

Aligning Universal Principles with Personal Values — *This exercise helps your daughter to incorporate universal principles with personal values.*

> Look over the universal principles in the earlier part of this chapter. Have your daughter pick three that she feels strongly about. Help her develop a plan of action that embraces each principle. For example, if she chooses "Harmony and Balance: Living in Tune with Nature," you may want to help her start a recycling project. If she chooses "The Golden Rule: The Relationship Adage," you and she might take time to help someone in your community. Let her decide how involved she wants to be.

Chapter Five

CHOICES

Building with the Hammer of Making Decisions

"The most difficult thing is the decision to act, the rest is merely tenacity. The fears are paper tigers. You can do anything you decide to do. You can act to change and control your life; and the procedure, the process is its own reward."
— Robyn Davidson

Since the Stone Age, people have continually searched for methods and tools that would make their lives easier. They found that rudimentary stone tools such as knives, hatchets, and hammers could help them kill their prey, prepare their food, and build their shelters. Just as prehistoric humans found that they could attach a wooden handle to a rock and do things more efficiently, people have used certain tools to help them make better decisions. The Connected Inner Guide is a tool that simplifies and enhances the decision-making process. It is the modern version of the prehistoric hammer.

The hammer of decision making, the Connected Inner Guide, shapes your daughter's choices with a balanced and integrated head, heart, and gut approach. The previous three chapters delved into these three components of the Connected Inner Guide and how they relate to each other. Your daughter must be in tune with these components and how they interact for the Connected Inner Guide to be used most effectively. Once she understands each component's function, she can bring them together to be an effective hammer of decision making. This chapter shows how this integrated tool, your daughter's Connected Inner Guide, becomes her hammer of decision making.

Regardless of your daughter's circumstances, her responses and decisions determine her success. In each decision she faces, there is a moment of choice. She can either let the Toxic Inner Critic, the Crybaby Heart, or the Creep take charge or she can victoriously choose to listen to her Comforter, Courageous Heart, and Trained Conscience. The choices that she makes directly affect her life and that of others. Each decision is better to the extent that she relies on her Connected Inner Guide, her hammer of decision making. Her Connected Inner Guide is her greatest resource in ensuring the success of her decisions.

BEN FRANKLIN'S "MORALS OF CHESS"

Integrity in the moment of choice is vital to a healthy Connected Inner Guide. Decision making is rarely easy. However, there are guidelines that can strengthen your daughter's success in this endeavor. In the essay "The Morals of Chess" by Benjamin Franklin, there are some valuable rules that can be applied to making sound decisions in life.

1. Foresight. Look ahead and consider the consequences of the action. Your daughter should base her foresight on reality, not on wishes.
2. Circumspection. Examine the whole picture, the relationships, the dangers, the possibilities, and the probabilities. This will increase your daughter's probability for a desirable outcome.
3. Caution. Don't make any move in haste. Observe the laws of the game — time-tested values and principles. Your daughter needs to understand that she must bear all the consequences of her actions.
4. Hope and Perseverance. Your daughter should not be discouraged by present mistakes. She should persevere in working toward better solutions.

These rules are as appropriate today as when they were written two hundred years ago. Foresight, circumspection, caution, hope, and perseverance all generate wisdom in the decision-making process. When your daughter's Connected Inner Guide applies these rules, her choices become clearer.

The Moment of Choice

"It is in your moments of decision that your destiny is shaped."
— Anthony Robbins

The effects of choices today are more complex than at any time in recent history. In the 1960s, a possible premature death due to an HIV infection was not a consequence of a sexual encounter. Today, it is. This brings a new and urgent importance to the decision-making process.

For teenagers, the decision-making process is complicated by the fact that their Comforter, Courageous Heart, and Trained Conscience are not yet fully developed. Impulsiveness, black-and-white thinking, and incomplete value systems all hinder the decision-making process. Author Leslie Kaplan notes in her book *Coping With Peer Pressure,* that making decisions is a process that requires patience, abstract thinking, and a deep awareness of personal values and priorities. Many times, teens are not equipped with these skills and suffer from lack of experience.

Making sound decisions is further complicated by many teens' inability to recognize realities in a situation. According to nationally syndicated Leonard Pitts, Jr., "teens live by wishes, making major decisions on the basis of what they want to be true, rather than what really is." Wishing is a futile activity. Wishing involves what might be, what is possible, what is desired, not what is. Making a decision based on a false reality is doomed to dismal failure, or at best, a random chance of success. A decision made in haste to beat the oncoming train across the track may result in the loss of life. A decision made in passion to engage in sex may have dire consequences both physically and emotionally. Many decisions have far-reaching effects. All decisions have consequences. Through an awareness of the reality, your daughter judges what is good or bad and, more important, what is best in each situation.

A stumbling block many parents face to putting "the hammer in her hand" — getting their adolescent daughter to use the Connected Inner Guide for decision making — is twofold:

- Because teens seek to form their own identity apart from their family, they may temporarily reject their parents' authority or advice.
- Teens' decisions are more complex than in previous times.

During the teen years, young girls begin the necessary and inevitable separation from the family. Adolescence is a time when they often attempt to thwart the constraints of the seemingly oppressive rules of their families, religion, and society. As they test the boundaries and often the notions of right and wrong, their actions may result in undesirable outcomes. This is an extremely trying time because they often refuse to take responsibility for their actions and behave as if consequences deferred are consequences escaped.

This "I can't worry about it today" attitude is characteristic of many teens. When tomorrow comes, teens may attempt to further delay the consequences or to deny them completely. The process of learning what is right is hampered by the misguided notion that a delay in the consequences can magically make the outcome of actions disappear.

In addition to facing the timeless trials and tribulations of separating from the family, teens are facing a second constraint — today's society. They face more difficult situations than previous generations. While most teens may be making sound decisions in general, one bad decision may have dire consequences. According to the *Congressional Quarterly,* the top disciplinary concerns in public schools in the 1940s were talking out of turn, chewing gum, making noise, running in the halls, cutting in line, dress code infractions, and littering. In the 1990s, these infractions were overshadowed by the pervasive problems of drug abuse, alcohol abuse, pregnancy, suicide, rape, robbery, and assault. A little compassion and empathy go a long way in showing your daughter that you understand that she is facing some difficult choices.

Not only are teens facing more difficult decisions, but they are also limited by their ability to understand many of the consequences of their actions. In *Self-Esteem,* McKay and Fanning state that this awareness of consequences is limited by five factors: ignorance, forgetting, denial, lack of alternatives, and habits.

- **Ignorance.** The first and most obvious factor is ignorance in a situation where the action has never been attempted. It is impossible to determine the consequences of a new, untried action. Only upon completion of an action can the consequences be known and a reasonable evaluation made. In your daughter's life, there are many untried actions. Experience is a great teacher but experience is lacking in the life of most teens. If your daughter is interested in making quality decisions, she can gain insight by examining the actions of others and learn from their mistakes.

- **Forgetting.** Many events have such minor consequences that they are not remembered and, as such, will probably be repeated. In the grand scheme of things, these actions require little thought and are easily forgotten. For example, your daughter may leave her raincoat at home on cloudy days and suffer an occasional drenching. If she is only in the rain for a short time or can quickly change out of her wet clothing, the discomfort is easily forgotten. She will probably forget her raincoat again because the consequences are not significant enough for her to remember and she will fail to alter her behavior.

- **Denial.** There are two causes of denial — fear and need. Some teens fear doing something so they minimize the consequences of avoiding it. Haley, a seventeen-year-old student at the High School for the Performing and Visual Arts, is like many teens who deny themselves opportunities based on fear. Haley had a chance to perform a solo at a tough dance competition. This competition afforded her the opportunity to compete against a much higher caliber of dancer than she had in the past. She also could be considered for possible college scholarships. But Haley was intimidated by the expertise of dancers she would compete against, was worried about failure, and sickened by the emphasis placed on this competition. Although this competition was critical, she decided to go to a party instead of practicing. Her justification to herself is that it was just another competition. In reality, her fear was the underlying factor motivating this poor decision. She should have weighed the positive and negative consequences of going to the party, but she didn't. And now, Haley's denial may have prevented her from a life-changing opportunity.

Another reason teens deny consequences is need. Some teens feel they need something so much that they deny the negative consequences of getting it. For instance, a teen might want a designer purse and resorts to shoplifting to obtain it. This unwise decision to shoplift carries consequences she fails to consider. The possibility of getting caught, the effect on her value system, the negative feelings that arise, and even the possibility that she might change her mind about wanting the purse all should be considered in her decision. Then, it will be clear to her that the negatives in this situation far outweigh the desire. If the need to have something is great enough to deny the consequences, then the reasoning behind this need must be examined and weighed. Need should not be the sole reason for a decision.

To avoid the limiting factor of denial when making a decision, your daughter must make a concentrated effort to become more aware of the reasons behind her decisions. When her reasoning is based on need or fear, your daughter must be aware that denial can obstruct her judgment.

- **Lack of alternatives.** Your daughter may simply not be aware of a better way to do something or may lack the experience, skill, or ability to work out a new solution. If there are no alternatives, your daughter must decide which action is better — doing something or doing nothing. It should be noted, however, that by not deciding she is making a decision.

- **Habits.** Some habits can prevent your daughter from evaluating or even being aware of the choices she has in a situation. This brings to mind the story about the young girl watching her mother prepare a pot roast for dinner. After her mother pulled out the big roasting pan she always used, she took a large knife and cut off the end of the meat. She then carefully placed both pieces in the pot end to end and surrounded the meat with carrots, potatoes, and onions. Curious, the young girl asked her mother why she cut the end off the roast. The mother unthinkingly replied, "Because that's the way I've always done it. And that's the way your grandmother did it." The young girl, still not satisfied, asked why again. Her mother thought for a moment and said, "I really don't know. Let's call Grandma." When they called the grandmother and asked her why, she replied, "So it will fit in my pan!" Habits are dangerous because they take the place of thought. Using the rationale "because that's the way I've always done it" may limit viable options in decision making.

Ignorance, forgetting, denial, lack of alternatives, and habits all can prevent sound decisions by omitting feasible options because of a lack of awareness. Any or all of these factors can limit your daughter's awareness of a decision's consequences. Teenagers are particularly vulnerable to these pitfalls because of their lack of experience.

Practicing awareness, and not unconsciously bumbling through life, is a choice. If your daughter makes a commitment to predict the consequences of her actions, she is less likely to fall prey to these factors that limit her awareness. She must evaluate the possible outcomes prior to any action for the action to be of benefit. As your daughter becomes more aware of the consequences in the moment of choice, she will become more competent in her decision making.

With each decision, a defining moment of choice for your daughter can make all the difference. Pearl S. Buck, winner of the 1938 Nobel Prize in literature, once noted that "every great mistake has a halfway moment, a split second when it can be recalled and perhaps remedied." Whether it is a split second or a lengthy interval, this moment gives your daughter the power to define her character by her decisions. By listening to the healthy components of her head, heart, and gut, your daughter can gain insight, compassion, and character with each decision. Her Connected Inner Guide is indispensable in this moment of choice.

OLD HABITS ARE HARD TO UPROOT

There is an old folk tale that emphasizes the importance of dealing quickly with bad habits. A young man planted a small thorn bush in the middle of a road. The king came upon it and ordered the man to remove it. The young man agreed but stated that he would remove it later. The years passed and the bush grew and the young man aged. Finally, the king returned and again ordered the man to remove the bush. The once young man feebly approached the bush only to find the bush too large to be easily removed and that he was too weak to remove it.

Bad habits, like the thorn bush, are best broken before they are firmly entrenched and too big to handle.

Filters: Screening Out Debris

"The circumstances that surround a man or woman's life are not important.
It is how the individual responds to those circumstances that is the number one
determining factor in whether they will fail or succeed." — Booker T. Washington

A filter is a useful tool that allows your daughter to strain out the undesirable elements in her life, while absorbing the positive. By using a filter, she can set a predetermined reaction in place that helps her decide what she wants to do, how she wants to do it, and with whom. Her filter eliminates the need to make a decision in the heat of the moment and reduces repetitive decision making.

A filter minimizes decision making by implementing previously decided limits. Filters can only be set by foresight. In implementing filters, your daughter considers probable situations she might face and determines how she will respond. This predetermined response becomes her filter.

A filter assists your daughter in decision making in two ways: It acts to shield out the undesirable debris that can confuse her decisions, and it allows in only the relevant factors that affect the decision.

Four types of filters are used to facilitate decision making: a previous experience filter, a minimum expectation filter, a maximum allowance filter, and a personal expectation filter.

Your daughter sets *previous experience filters* based on lessons she has learned from past events. When thoughts or actions prove to be detrimental, she establishes a response that keeps her from reexperiencing the negative consequences of an action. Or when past thoughts or actions prove to be beneficial, she establishes a response accordingly. Because the filter is established, decision making is kept to a minimum — what is desirable and what is damaging is already determined. Her decision is in place.

Kaitlyn, an astute sixteen-year-old, set a personal experience filter for making decisions. After her uncle was killed because of driving while intoxicated, Kaitlyn decided to establish a filter of not allowing her friends to drink and drive. (The filter is "no drinking and driving.") While at a party, her friend Sam participated in a drinking game. She knew that he intended to drive home, but Kaitlyn's filter was already in place. She had already decided not to let her friend drink and drive. She did not have to struggle with the question "What should I do?" Because she set this filter, Kaitlyn's only decision was to drive him home or find him a ride.

A filter may also dictate what your daughter will accept in her life. There is a minimum tolerance for what she expects from others and a maximum tolerance for what she will allow. Her *minimum expectation filter* is the least she is willing to accept from a situation or a person. For example, loyalty is one of Allison's minimum requirements for friendship. Allison needed advice about a confidential matter, so she privately discussed it with her friend Rachel. Rachel told the secret, causing Allison to doubt her loyalty. Allison must now reevaluate her friendship with Rachel or adjust her minimum expectation filter.

A *maximum allowance filter* is a ceiling on what your daughter will accept from a situation or person. Your daughter might set a filter that she will only put up with her friend's tardiness until it makes her late for school. When her friend Emily is late again, your daughter realizes that she will be late to school. Your daughter has a preset filter in place, so she does not have to struggle with the decision of "What should I do about my friend being late?" She finds another ride.

Your daughter's *personal expectation filter* identifies her personal level of expectations for herself. These are the standards and limits your daughter places on her thoughts and actions, based on her healthy Connected Inner Guide — her Comforter's insight, her Courageous Heart's feelings, and her Trained Conscience's values and principles.

These filters act as tools to enable your daughter to control what she allows in her life. Her filters should align with her Connected Inner Guide's wisdom. The filters she has set in place are malleable as her Connected Inner Guide matures. If a young girl values money, she might set a filter that she will only be friends with rich kids. As she realizes that money isn't everything, she adjusts her filter to be more inclusive. If her values change, so will her filters. Her filters are uniquely hers. By presetting decision filters, your daughter can minimize the number of decisions she makes under stress and can reduce repetitive decisions.

Tips from the Toolbox

These questions can help your daughter set filters:

- *In the past year, think of a decision that you made. Were you pleased with the outcome? What would you do differently, if faced with a similar problem? Can you put a filter in place now that will aid in making a sound decision in the future?*
- *Now, recall a situation where you felt used by a friend. What were your actions? Were you satisfied with the outcome? Would setting a tolerance level have helped? Do you have the same requirements for yourself that you expect from your friends and parents? Do you need to change your personal expectation filter?*

Mistakes: The Drawing Board

"In fact, I have learned more from my defeats than from my victories. I would advise young women to be willing to take risks — and to risk failure."
— Senator Kay Bailey Hutchison

Each decision is a learning process into what works and what doesn't. Despite adherence to the rules of decision making and an awareness of the consequences, mistakes will be made. This is a fact of life. In addition to integrity in the moment of choice and filters, mistakes can be another useful tool to assist the Connected Inner Guide in making decisions. Mistakes, if viewed appropriately, are the drawing board to reengineer decisions to be successful. Henry Ford once remarked, "Even a mistake may turn out to be the one thing necessary to a worthwhile achievement." He understood that mistakes are lessons along the path to success.

Because mistakes are inevitable, they should not be avoided, feared, or viewed as failure. They are necessary steps in the learning process. Mistakes provide information needed to tailor future decisions. They serve as guidelines or warnings. For instance, a low C in a course may mean your daughter needs to study more or get extra help. A dented car fender may mean she needs to readjust the mirror or pay closer attention while driving.

Basically, what really matters is that your daughter make the best decision at the time based on the information available. She should take personal responsibility for the mistake and learn from it. It is okay to disappoint people or have awkward moments. Your daughter should understand that mistakes have nothing to do with self-worth or intelligence. McKay and Fanning, authors of *Self-Esteem*, say it best: "Feeling good about yourself is not something that you do after all mistakes have been corrected — it's something you do in spite of mistakes." The only real failure for your daughter is letting her Toxic Inner Critic tell her that mistakes are evidence of worthlessness. If she makes the necessary corrections and stores the information for future reference, her future decisions can benefit from the error.

When your daughter learns to view the decision-making process as a work in progress, she does not have to be overly harsh on herself because of mistakes. When mistakes prevent her from venturing out and trying new ideas, they can be traps that keep her from learning and growing. Mistakes should be a teacher, not a jailer.

A SIX-POINT TEST FOR DECIDING RIGHT FROM WRONG

Quoted from noted clergyman and author Dr. Harry Emerson Fosdick.

1. Does the course of action you plan to follow seem logical and reasonable? Never mind what anyone else has to say. Does it make sense to you? If it does, it is probably right.
2. Does it pass the test of sportsmanship? In other words, if everyone followed this same course of action, would the results be beneficial for all?
3. Where will your plan of action lead? How will it affect others? What will it do to you?
4. Will you think well of yourself when you look at what you have done?
5. Try to separate yourself from the problem. Pretend, for one moment, it is the problem of the person you most admire. Ask yourself how that person would handle it.
6. Hold up the final decision to the glaring light of publicity. Would you want your family and friends to know what you have done? The decisions we make in the hope that no one will find out are usually wrong.

Personal Responsibility

"In the last analysis, the individual person is responsible for living his own life and for finding himself. If he persists in shifting his responsibility to somebody else, he fails to find out the meaning of his own existence." — Thomas Merton

Entire societies depend on the family and on personal responsibility. Edward Gibbon, a noted historian, identifies five main causes for the decline and fall of the Roman Empire. The top two reasons on his list are the breakdown of the family structure and the weakening of a sense of individual responsibility.

Strong families are crucial in the survival of societies and are paramount in the teaching of ethics and values. It is the family that teaches personal responsibility best. As a parent, your job is to help your daughter develop personal responsibility. If you don't, someone else will. Although you cannot directly change her, you can be a resource, available to nurture, encourage, and support her responsible behavior.

Personal responsibility involves the willingness to accept the consequences of personal actions. It involves following through with commitments and obligations. Giving your daughter the ability to choose affirms her individual responsibility. Allowing her to feel in control affirms her self-worth. When parents give their daughters choices and control over their actions, it opens the door to self-direction based on self-discipline.

True personal responsibility incorporates accountability. It means accepting responsibility, making the best choice possible, and then standing by the decision after it is made. It requires your daughter to accept the consequences of her own actions. Responsible daughters don't pass the buck. They don't blame others or make excuses.

Deflecting the blame can rob your daughter of many growth experiences. It is easy to place blame elsewhere, but it is counterproductive. If she blames others for her mistakes, she fails to learn the lessons imparted by them. Taking responsibility for mistakes is a part of the empowerment of adulthood.

Although your daughter can learn from a mistake and forgive herself, she still should hold herself personally accountable for any harm she may have caused. Her mistakes should incorporate accountability. When your daughter understands that she and no one else creates what goes on in her head, heart, and gut, then she will make necessary choices and accept their consequences.

Tips from the Toolbox

Your daughter needs to understand when and where she has failed to take responsibility so she can correct it. If you constantly point out her shortcomings, though, you will risk alienating her. A better approach is to refer to the Connected Inner Guide as a help in accepting responsibility. The best decisions are made with the Comforter of the head, the Courageous Heart of the heart, and the Trained Conscience of the gut. It will be much easier for her to stand behind and take responsibility for her decisions when she makes them using her Connected Inner Guide.

Exaggerations and Imbalances of the Connected Inner Guide

"We can be sure that the greatest hope for maintaining equilibrium in the face of any situation rests within ourselves. Persons who are secure with a transcendental system of values and a deep sense of moral duties are possessors of values which no man and no catastrophe can take from them." — Dr. Francis J. Braceland

When any one component of the Connected Inner Guide wields too much control, it is always at the expense of the other components, and more important, sound decisions. The takeover or surrender of any component of the decision-making centers (the head, the heart, and the gut) upsets the crucial balance of the Connected Inner Guide. This imbalance jeopardizes sound decisions and turns your daughter's Connected Inner Guide, the hammer in her hand, into formless, powerless metal.

The surrender or takeover of one component forces a misalignment in the Connected Inner Guide. This causes the Connected Inner Guide to disregard sound reasoning, emotional stability, or personal values. Often, this empowers the other negative components of the Connected Inner Guide to initiate an assault on the decision-making process.

When the Toxic Inner Critic, the Crybaby Heart, and the Creep team up, they are much more difficult to combat. When working together, they can convince each other that they know what is best in a situation. If your daughter lets these bad components of the Connected Inner Guide join forces, they can destroy sound decision making.

The story of Ashley, a somewhat insecure thirteen-year-old, illustrates how the bad components of the Connected Inner Guide can team up to damage decision-making power. Ashley believes all the popular kids are smoking marijuana after school, and she desperately wants to be accepted. Ashley goes along with the crowd, abandoning her values and discernment. Her Connected Inner Guide tells her this is wrong, but she allows her desire to be popular at all cost to govern her decision instead. Her Toxic Inner Critic uses the distortion of all-or-nothing thinking to belittle her by saying, "You won't be popular if you don't hang out with this group." Her Crybaby Heart adds fear to the assessment by saying, "You won't get another chance to be included, if you don't go along with them." Her Creep chimes in, "Nobody will find out. Just this once won't hurt." Together, these components' arguments are hard to negate, but not impossible to defeat.

Ashley can overcome these destructive components of the Connected Inner Guide by enlisting the help of her Comforter, her Courageous Heart, or her Trained Conscience. Any one of these positive components can start the process to making a better decision. Her Trained Conscience can say, "This is wrong, and it is against the law." Her Courageous Heart can remind her, "Doing something wrong doesn't make you happy or popular." Her Comforter can act as her ally by adding logic to the decision and affirming, "True friends don't require you to do anything stupid." When the positive components of the Connected Inner Guide team up, they become the healthy Connected Inner Guide. Working in harmony and balance, they bring wisdom, courage, and integrity to the decision-making process.

Ten Strategies to Make Better Decisions

The Connected Inner Guide is your daughter's hammer in her hand, her decision-making tool. When she relies on and develops this trusted tool, she incorporates strength and personal responsibility into her decisions. Also, her confidence is built up or torn down incrementally with each decision. She must remember that her actions always have consequences, and the decision to act or not should always account for these consequences. Below are some strategies that can aid your daughter's Connected Inner Guide in making better decisions:

1. **Practice integrity in the moment of choice.** This requires your daughter to pause before making a decision and consider the consequences.
2. **Plan responses to anticipated decisions.** When your daughter plans her reactions ahead of time, she can reduce the stress and time required to decide. By using preset filters, she has already considered the consequences and determined the best response.
3. **Collect as much information as possible when making a decision.** Your daughter may want to consult others who have faced similar situations. She may want to read autobiographies of strong women or specific information pertaining to her decision. The more information she can gather, the better the chance of her making a sound decision.
4. **View decision making like a chess game.** Examine all the foreseeable scenarios and track where each decision will lead and what follows.

5. **Evaluate past decisions and their consequences.** Your daughter can learn a lot from her past mistakes and successes.

6. **Prioritize what is important.** Your daughter needs to understand she may have to forgo a good decision for a better one.

7. **Become personally responsible for your actions.** Your daughter's personal responsibility means holding herself accountable for her decisions as well as the consequences associated with them.

8. **Don't be afraid to make a decision.** Your daughter should remember that not acting is a decision also.

9. **Start today to eliminate bad habits that inhibit sound decision making.** The sooner your daughter stops allowing the negative components of the Connected Inner Guide to govern her decisions, the better her outcomes will be.

10. **Practice, practice, practice.** Your daughter should use her Connected Inner Guide even in small decisions. Remember, your daughter's best tool in decision making is her Connected Inner Guide.

Your daughter builds strength and confidence as she converts the Toxic Inner Critic into the Comforter, the Crybaby Heart into the Courageous Heart, and the Creep into the Trained Conscience. As these transformations occur, the Comforter, the Courageous Heart, and the Trained Conscience interact to bring a whole, integrated guide to the decision-making process. No matter what situation your daughter faces, her decisions, her choices shape the quality of her life. The time she chooses to invest in developing her hammer of decision making will be time well spent.

The hammer of decision making is indispensable to shape your daughter's life and give her direction. However, as vital as the hammer of decision making is, it is not the only tool that your daughter needs in her toolbox. There are additional proven life skills that build the fortitude necessary to face life's challenges. The next chapter examines these "power tools," time-tested life skills that will help your daughter gain the wisdom and perspective that lead to her success and happiness.

HONING THE SKILLS
What You Can Do

Viewing Mistakes as Teachers — *This internal exercise helps you appreciate mistakes as learning opportunities.*

How do you view mistakes? How do you view your daughter's mistakes? What signals are you sending? Are mistakes okay? Is your attitude toward your daughter based on her performance? Do you praise her for trying, regardless of success? To understand the benefit of mistakes, realize that everyone makes mistakes — even you. Make a list of people that you respect and some of their mistakes. Note what you can learn from these mistakes.

What You Can Do with Your Older Daughter (Ages Thirteen to Twenty-Three)

Learning Personal Responsibility — *This exercise helps your daughter assess how responsible she is.*

By examining these questions, your daughter can develop awareness of her personal responsibility and accountability:

■ Do you take personal responsibility and hold yourself accountable for your actions or do you blame others?
■ To whom are you accountable? Your God? Yourself? Your parents? Others?
■ Can you think of mistakes that you have made that you did not accept responsibility for?

Make a commitment to accept responsibility for future similar situations.

Facing the Critical Moment of Choice — *This activity will help your daughter develop an awareness with each decision.*

> Make a promise to each other to become more conscious of each decision that you make. Every time you face a decision, pause and think how you will respond to the choices you have. Pause in the moment of choice and analyze the factors that are acting upon you. Are you listening to your Crybaby Heart and acting in frustration? Are you deciding based on only one component of the Connected Inner Guide at the expense of the others, such as letting your Toxic Inner Critic have too much power and not listening to your Courageous Heart or Trained Conscience? With each moment of choice, you have the option to let your healthy Connected Inner Guide direct decisions.

Keeping the Connected Inner Guide in Balance — *This exercise will help your daughter recognize the harm of letting one component of the Connected Inner Guide dominate.*

> Start a conversation with your daughter about how people can make the wrong decision by letting their emotions take over. Try to discuss specific incidents that you recall. Don't react judgmentally — keep the doors of communication open. As you discuss these examples, help your daughter recognize that people have fewer regrets when they act according to a Connected Inner Guide.

What You Can Do with Your Younger Daughter (Ages Six to Twelve)

Dealing with Bad Habits — *This activity helps your daughter see how habits can become too big to handle.*

> Relate the story on page 122 to your daughter about the thorn bush and the importance of dealing with bad habits quickly. Have both of you think about some habits you need to break. Develop a plan of action to correct them.

Understanding Filters— *Here is an exercise that will help your young daughter understand what a filter does.*

> Look around the house and find a window screen, a colander, or a tea strainer to use as a filter. Select sand, gravel, or pebbles. If this is not convenient, use sugar, dried peas, or rice. Sift these through the filter. Note what passes through and what does not. Explain how the filter kept some of the elements out. Review pages 122–124 about filters. Now, in terms of decision making, discuss with your daughter how you can predetermine responses by setting filters that can simplify decisions.

Chapter Six

THE POWER TOOLS

"We cannot change our past. . . . We cannot change the fact that people will act in a certain way. We cannot change the inevitable. The only thing we can do is play on the string we have, and that is our attitude. . . . I am convinced that life is 10 percent what happens to me and 90 percent how I react to it. And so it is with you. . . . We are in charge of our attitudes."
— Charles Swindoll

Building a quality life depends on meticulous craftsmanship and perseverance. This arduous undertaking is a work in progress that requires continuous construction. Diligent and conscientious work creates a sound structure of strength — an inner fortress where your daughter can stand self-assured and protected, a place where she can replenish, reinforce, and rest.

Building this quality life is labor intensive, but the process can be simplified using the correct tools. Hand tools are sufficient for minor projects. However, a major project requires more power. Life is a major project. This major undertaking requires investing in quality power tools. Your daughter is worth this investment.

Young women can build decision-making skills with the hammer of decision making, the Connected Inner Guide. In addition to this practical tool, we would equip our daughters with a toolbox fitted with time-tested, powerful tools for success. We would place in each of their toolboxes power tools and tell them, "Dig deep. Build high. Stand strong. You are worth it."

The power tools are proven techniques to build the fortitude necessary to face life's challenges. These tools can be implemented today and used throughout life. While these tools can be used without added power, they are more effective with a current of optimism.

Your daughter is building a sanctuary of inner peace, self-esteem, and happiness. She must continually build up, tear down, and remodel this inner fortress to adjust for life's challenges. She needs these power tools, fueled by optimism, to equip her with valuable life skills and techniques.

Pragmatic Optimism

"Optimism: The fuel of heroes, the enemy of despair, the creator of the future."
— Max More, Ph.D.

The current of optimism energizes and optimizes the power tools to build strength and self-worth. Pragmatic optimism in two words is "I can." This "I can" attitude is a learned and powerful technique for dealing with difficulties in life. The "I can" attitude of pragmatic optimism is not only the force that charges the power tools but also may be the master key to healthy self-esteem.

You're probably thinking, "Oh, great. Here comes that trite Pollyanna mentality. Put on the old, rose-colored glasses and buy into the 'it will all work out okay' pipe dream."

Well, throw away those distorted glasses. Pragmatic optimism is not about luckily escaping misfortune or blindly viewing reality. It is not about hoping that someone else will make the future better. Pragmatic optimism is the belief that you can and will bring about what you want. It is a learned, active, motivating charge that drives the power tools. This optimism is not the blind faith of wishes and dreams. It is a pragmatic "I can" approach to life that takes responsibility for choices and their consequences.

Max More, Ph.D., philosopher and cofounder of Extropy, calls this force *dynamic optimism.* "Dynamic Optimism is an active, empowering, constructive attitude that creates conditions for success by focusing and acting on possibilities and opportunities. The dynamic optimist both interprets experience positively and influences outcomes positively." Dr. More developed the concept of dynamic optimism to integrate the motivating uplifting effects of optimism with an active, responsible approach to living. For optimism to give your daughter the power to overcome the limitations in her life, she needs to fully recognize reality, not hide from it. For optimism to maximize her abilities and happiness, she has to take responsibility for her thoughts, her attitudes, and her actions.

An excellent way to teach your daughter the "I can" attitude of pragmatic optimism is to model the behavior. Gail, a forty-three-year-old attorney, relates a story that demonstrates pragmatic optimism. While shopping with her daughter, Jennifer, Gail backed into a parking space, misjudging the distance. She dented the car next to her and scraped the paint off the side of her own car. Gail quickly looked around and realized no one was looking. She knew she could get away with it and pretend that the scrape on her car wasn't her fault. Gail's Toxic Inner Critic screamed, "Ignore the situation." Her Crybaby Heart whined, "Big trouble. Run while you can." Her Creep urged her, " Just lie about it."

After her initial thoughts, Gail took control of the situation and relied on the pragmatic optimism of the Connected Inner Guide to quiet the cognitive distortions of her Toxic Inner Critic, the whining emotions of her Crybaby Heart, and the amoral philosophy of her Creep. Her Connected Inner Guide responded, "This accident was my fault and I am responsible for correcting this problem. Whatever I have to do, I will." She knew modeling the appropriate behavior for her daughter meant taking charge of the situation and creating the conditions necessary for taking personal responsibility. Gail left a note on the dented car and contacted mall security with the details of the accident. Gail showed Jennifer that she could face the situation and handle its consequences. Her "I can" attitude taught Jennifer a valuable lesson.

Pragmatic optimism always involves deciding to face the situation, knowing that you can handle the consequences. Your daughter can learn positive skills to develop pragmatic optimism, even if she does not consider herself an optimistic person.

In his book *Learned Optimism,* Martin Seligman discusses his research showing that optimism is a skill anyone can master. Seligman, one of the world's experts on motivation, tracked ten- to twelve-year-olds at risk for depression. They were taught skills to dispute negative thoughts and to negotiate with peers. Of the moderately depressed participants, 44 percent of those not taught the coping skills became even more depressed, while only 20 percent of those taught coping skills showed an increase in depression. This comprehensive study demonstrates that skills can be learned to dispute negative thoughts and better face life's challenges.

Your daughter can learn skills such as pragmatic optimism to overcome negative thinking. This pragmatic optimism is the current your Connected Inner Guide uses to fuel the power tools. The lists that follow can help you explain pragmatic optimism to your daughter by contrasting "I can" thoughts with negative "I can't" thoughts.

"I Can" People

- Listen to their Connected Inner Guide's wisdom
- Attribute failure to temporary causes and favorable situations to lasting causes
- Don't let one setback contaminate their whole life
- Feel they are in charge of their life
- Persist in the face of failure because they believe in themselves
- Have a sense of abundance, recognizing the world to be full of opportunities
- Attend to the downside of life only to the extent that it will enable them to move ahead
- Take the world as it is, not complaining that life is not fair
- Are open to new, feasible possibilities
- View others' success as a model to learn from
- Are proactive rather than reactive
- Dwell on the constructive and the enjoyable while de-emphasizing the pain, difficulty, and frustration

"I CAN'T" PEOPLE

- Buy into the Toxic Inner Critic's distortions, dote on the Crybaby Heart's exaggerated emotions, and give in to the Creep's amoral philosophy
- Believe bad events stem from permanent conditions and good from temporary ones
- Allow one disappointment to pervade their whole life
- Feel helpless, and therefore, hopeless
- Give up easily, often before beginning a challenge
- See the world as full of obstacles and empty of options
- Allow the negatives in life to prevent progress
- Whine, criticize, and blame
- Accept limits without question, feeling comfortable with the given, lacking the drive to search for solutions
- View others' success as a threat to their own chance of success
- React passively (sleep through it) or are volatile (knee-jerk reaction)
- Focus on problems, pains, and pitfalls

One of the fascinating features of pragmatic optimism is that it incrementally builds on itself. V. M. Parachin states in his article, "Ten Steps to Self-Esteem," in *Your Health* magazine, "Optimistic thinking is the surest way of creating an upward cycle, moving from one success to another and building greater self-esteem.... A key step to greater self-esteem is to adopt the stance of being a confident, happy, successful person; you can grow into a role. Individuals with strong self-esteem do not give up easily; they learn from mistakes and let failure drive them to do better the next time."

Remember the story of *The Little Engine That Could* and her relentless determination to keep trying despite failures — "I think I can, I think I can.... I *knew* I could, I *knew* I could!" Her "I can" attitude of optimism produced the victory. Just such a current of optimism provides a powerful force to change the way your daughter views situations, takes on responsibility, and fosters her happiness. Your daughter's Connected Inner Guide requires pragmatic optimism to fuel the power tools.

The following are the power tools and techniques that can help your daughter live a more fulfilled life

- Adjusting Your Mirror — visualizing the best you can be through mirror talk
- Designing Your Lifetime Strategic Plan — creating and implementing a plan for your life
- Expanding Your Limits — calculating your strengths and weaknesses and forging ahead
- Experiencing the Humor — letting humor heal physically and emotionally
- Gratitude — unearthing the hidden treasures of gratitude and awareness
- Cultivating Unconditional Love — forming a culture of unconditional love for yourself and others
- Resting in Spirituality — listening to your soul

The "I Can" Attitude

- Keeps events in proportion
- Looks forward
- Focuses on the positive
- Sets realistic goals and standards
- Associates with positive people
- Promotes personal growth

These power tools are proven techniques that will build the fortitude necessary for your daughter to face life's challenges. Your daughter can learn many of these tools by your modeling them. Others will require sitting down with your daughter and working through them over a period of time. When your daughter's Connected Inner Guide incorporates these power tools fueled by pragmatic optimism, she can reach her true potential. As you explore these life skills with your daughter, keep in mind that these tools can be applied immediately and used throughout life.

The Power Tool of Adjusting Your Mirror

"It's the repetition of affirmations that leads to belief. And once that belief becomes a deep conviction, things begin to happen." — Claude M. Bristol

The mind is a powerful mechanism that dramatically impacts self-worth. It starts with a thought and creates its own reality. How your daughter sees herself to a great extent determines who she is. Just as she looks in the mirror daily and sees her reflection, her mind reinforces a mental picture of how she sees herself. It reinforces this image with either criticism or praise. If she has a negative-self image, she can learn to change the way she views herself. She can "adjust her mirror" with mirror talk to create the person she wants to be.

Norman Vincent Peale, a proponent of positive imaging, got a standing ovation when he addressed a professional group and sagely noted, "There is a deep tendency in human nature ultimately to become precisely what you visualize yourself as being. If you see yourself as tense and nervous and frustrated, if that is your image of yourself, that assuredly is what you will be. If you see yourself as inferior in any way, and you hold that image in your conscious mind, it will presently by the process of intellectual osmosis sink into the unconscious, and you will be what you visualize. If, on the contrary, you see yourself as organized, controlled, studious, a thinker, a worker, believing in your talent and ability and yourself, over a period of time, that is what you will become."

A parable by Anthony de Mello called "The Golden Eagle" emphasizes the power of visualization — you are what you think you are.

> Once there was a man who found an eagle's egg and put it in the nest of a backyard hen. The eaglet hatched with the brood of chicks and grew up with them.
>
> All his life, the eagle did what the backyard chickens did, thinking he was a backyard chicken. He scratched the earth for

worms and insects. He clucked and cackled. And he would thrash his wings and fly a few feet into the air.

Years passed and the eagle grew very old. One day, he saw a magnificent bird far above him in the cloudless sky. It glided in graceful majesty among the powerful wind currents, with scarcely a beat of its strong golden wings.

The old eagle looked up in awe. "Who's that?" he asked.

"That's the eagle, the king of the birds," said his neighbor. "He belongs to the sky. We belong to the earth — we're chickens."

So the eagle lived and died a chicken for that's what he thought he was.

The eagle's failure to adjust his mirror completely changed his life. He based his concept of himself on others and did not fulfill his true nature. If he had only visualized himself as the great and powerful bird that he was, he would have become the eagle that he was meant to be.

Your daughter may base her opinion of herself on others' opinions of her, but this may not be her true identity. It is possible for her to change her concept of herself by adjusting her mirror. She has a choice — she can be satisfied with the chicken's image if she is a chicken, but if she is an eagle, she has drastically shortchanged herself.

 Tips from the Toolbox

How do you view your daughter? Do you fail to notice some of her attributes because they are not as obvious as another child's? Are you shortchanging your daughter by not recognizing these strengths? Are you dwelling on some of her strengths at the expense of others? You may be slighting your daughter by not viewing the whole picture. How you view your daughter influences how she views herself.

The mind's strength is formidable, as you have seen in the Toxic Inner Critic's attempts to corrupt the Connected Inner Guide. The Toxic Inner Critic uses derogatory voices to create a negative self-image that undermines confidence. This invisible, pervasive force squelches self-esteem, continually battling the Comforter for control of how your daughter sees herself.

The Comforter is the voice that your daughter uses to adjust her mental picture. The Comforter uses pragmatic optimism to tell her that she is good enough and she can succeed. It urges her to take risks and develop her capabilities to the fullest. Just as she sees herself in the mirror, her mind visualizes the picture that the Comforter creates. The Comforter can adjust her mirror to create the person she wants to be.

If your daughter doesn't see herself as a good, positive, loving person, then how can she be one? She must allow the Comforter to adjust her mirror often. It is critical that she develop a strong, positive belief in herself and her capabilities. Continuous realignment of her mirror helps her keep in focus the type of person she desires to be.

If she is unhappy with the image of herself that her mind creates, the "I can" attitude of pragmatic optimism can help. Like the Little Engine That Could, if she thinks she can, she can. When she is unhappy with her mental picture, she must realign her mirror. After all, if she were perfect, there would be no room for personal growth. Putting negative thoughts into perspective allows her to positively examine the characteristics that need her attention. This enables her to move forward and adjust her mental image. Pragmatic optimism makes aligning her mirror easier.

Aligning the mirror is extremely effective in promoting self-worth and creating a positive self-image. The Comforter, using pragmatic optimism, creates this picture of self-worth. It accepts your daughter as she is and uses "mirror talk" to direct her toward a better image.

Early in his career, heavyweight boxer Muhammad Ali proclaimed boldly, "I am the greatest!" His assertion became reality as he won the heavyweight boxing championship title. Long before he obtained his crown, he believed in the power of his proclamation. He believed in himself. He saw himself as a champion and therefore he was. By making a tangible positive affirmation, he changed his life. Like Ali, the Comforter can use positive affirmations, or mirror talk, with dramatic results.

Mirror talk is a statement that, through the act of repetition, becomes implanted in the mind. Mirror talk allows your daughter's Comforter to adjust her self-image or mirror. By using mirror talk, she changes negative and unproductive thoughts into positive, mirror-adjusting beliefs. With regular practice, she creates her desired self-image, and this image becomes reality.

How to Make Mirror Talk More Effective

Here are some proven ways, according to Jeffrey Staniforth in his "Guide to Affirmations," that can help your daughter make mirror talk more effective:

1. **Use present tense.** Your daughter's mirror talk is more effective when it is stated in the present tense. For example, instead of "I will become responsible for my life," affirm "I am responsible for my life." She should avoid stating her mirror talk in the future tense, or the results always will be waiting to happen.

2. **Be positive.** Your daughter should create her mirror talk in the most positive terms that she can, avoiding negative statements. She should state what she does want, rather than what she does not want. "I don't want to make bad grades" (a negative statement), is made more effective by affirming "I now enjoy being a good student." This statement is more powerful because it is positive and reinforces the desired goal.

3. **Keep it short and specific.** Short mirror talk is easy to say and has a greater impact at a subconscious level than statements that are long and wordy. Your daughter should say her mirror talk clearly and slowly. It should be specific and to the point. This adds power.

4. **Use repetition.** The importance of repetition cannot be overemphasized. It imprints the mirror talk into your daughter's subconscious mind.

5. **Involve the emotions.** Your daughter must be passionate and use the emotions of the Courageous Heart when she practices her mirror talk. It is helpful to think carefully about the meaning of the words rather than parroting them unconsciously.

6. **Be persistent.** Persistence in mirror talk achieves results much sooner. Your daughter's repeated sessions have a greater impact.

7. **Nurture belief.** Your daughter doesn't necessarily have to believe her affirmations initially. If she feels the power behind the words, belief will grow with repeated sessions of mirror talk.

8. **Use personalization for empowerment.** Your daughter should personalize her mirror talk to feel right for her. The stronger the

mirror talk, the deeper the impression it makes on her mind, and the sooner she will experience positive results.

The key to mirror talk is repetitive practice. Your daughter's mirror talk is unique to her personality and will change as her situation changes. Whatever mirror talk she chooses to adopt, she has the power to create exactly who she wants to be. Mirror talk is a power tool fueled with optimism to enhance her self-worth.

Mirror talk allows the Comforter to adjust your daughter's self-image or mirror. Through the act of repetition, mirror talk becomes implanted in the mind. The power of mirror talk is limited only by her personal conviction and belief that the mirror talk is working. By using mirror talk, your daughter changes negative and unproductive thoughts into positive, mirror-adjusting beliefs. And with regular practice, she has the power tool to become the best she can be.

Tips from the Toolbox

There are many ways for your daughter to practice mirror talk.

- *Suggest that your daughter write her mirror talk down and place it on her mirror or bulletin board, sing it to a favorite tune, or adopt her own theme song.*

- *Mirror talk that works is repetitive, so she might try linking it with a routine task like brushing her teeth or washing her hands.*

- *It helps to set aside a certain time each day for mirror talk. If she is a morning person, her mirror talk may work best when she first wakes up and her mind is more receptive. If she decides evening is better, as she winds down from the day, repeating her mirror talk will carry her visualization on a subconscious level while she sleeps.*

- *She should keep her mirror talk readily available so that she can refer to it often and update it as needed.*

- *She can keep her old lists of mirror talk to see how many of her affirmations become reality.*

MIRROR TALK: REFLECTING THE BEST YOU

Your daughter can use this list to customize her mirror talk to fit her needs or she can write her own.

I love myself, mistakes and all.

I am responsible for my body.

I am a worthwhile person.

I am beautiful inside and out.

I am a child of God.

I deserve to be loved by myself and others.

I am successful in many ways.

I forgive myself for hurting myself and others.

I will not let others hurt me.

I choose integrity in the moment of choice.

I am whole and good.

I celebrate my small victories.

I expand my limits.

I have a pioneering spirit.

I am thankful.

I appreciate humor.

I am capable of changing.

I value my Connected Inner Guide's wisdom.

My Comforter controls my Toxic Inner Critic.

My Courageous Heart silences my Crybaby Heart.

My Trained Conscience defeats my Creep.

I always do the best I can.

I am basically all right as I am.

I accept the consequences of my actions.

No one is more or less worthy than I.

I learn from my mistakes.

I invent new ways to satisfy needs and wisely choose the best option.

I care for and use my power tools to build and protect my self-esteem.

My future begins now.

The Power Tool of Designing Your Lifetime Strategic Plan

"Your vision will become clear only when you can look into your own heart: who looks outside dreams; who looks inside, awakes." — Carl Jung

It is easy for your daughter to lose track of who she is and where she is going in the day-to-day busyness of life. A Lifetime Strategic Plan is a powerful tool of awareness that can keep her focused on who she is and where she is going. Just as an airplane pilot is responsible for his flight plan, your daughter is responsible for her own course, or Lifetime Strategic Plan. Designing this Lifetime Strategic Plan is a process of developing a long-term, holistic course of action to guide her toward her vision and her goals. This plan incorporates a view of the big picture, a direction, and a strategy to take her to her destination. The Lifetime Strategic Plan, like the flight plan, not only focuses on the destination, but also on its path. Both plans include specific steps to achieve the objective. Your daughter cannot land without taking off. She cannot reach her destination if she goes in the wrong direction. Each step is necessary to arrive at her intended place. These steps help make her plan more manageable.

If your daughter doesn't determine where she wants to go, how can she possibly get there? Designing Your Lifetime Strategic Plan is a powerful tool, a proven technique that will help your daughter develop a lifetime sense of who she is, where she is going, and how she plans to get there. You can be instrumental in helping her in this endeavor. The power tool of Designing Your Lifetime Strategic Plan includes knowing who you are (the mission statement), who you want to become (the vision), and how you are going to accomplish this (the activity plan).

The Mission Statement: Who Are You?

Mary Kay Ash, founder of Mary Kay Cosmetics, built an empire based on her mission. Not only did she want to have a prosperous business, but she also wanted women to succeed. In her book *Mary Kay: On People Management*, she states, "I had a product and I had the drive and energy to make my business successful, but I wanted one more thing. . . . I wanted to help women achieve." Mary Kay Ash knew who she was — a woman who had drive and energy and the motivation for women to succeed. This mission was the ultimate empowerer, giving purpose to her life, adding meaning and passion to what she would accomplish.

A clear, concise mission statement defines for your daughter who she is and what she does. It has passion, humanity, and an eye for the big picture. Your daughter can find purpose and reason for her existence within her mission statement.

She may not realize that she has a mission statement, but she has one. An awareness of her mission statement is a pivotal point in developing her Lifetime Strategic Plan. Articulating who she is and her purpose adds cognitive control to her life.

Your daughter's mission enables her to focus on what truly matters and assists her Connected Inner Guide in prioritizing her decisions. It forces her to clarify and express succinctly her deepest values and aspirations.

Integrating mirror talk into your daughter's personal mission statement provides a logical place to start in forming her mission statement. Her mirror talk already incorporates pragmatic optimism for her to create a positive self-image. By using mirror talk affirmations, she has the basis for a valid mission statement. Her mission statement gives her a way to keep her focus constantly before her. When she repeats her mission statement over time, like mirror talk, it becomes a part of her, rather than something she just thinks about occasionally.

To develop a Lifetime Strategic Plan, you first create a personal mission statement. You may want to schedule a time for you and your daughter to work on your own personal mission statements. Mission statements require a lot of thought about who you are and how you see yourself. Writing these statements, in the following five steps, helps to focus and clarify your and your daughter's goals and aspirations.

Step One. You and your daughter wear a variety of hats in your lives — in your family, community, school, sports, work, church, or other organizations.

Both of you need to define how you would like to be described in these roles. Are there common threads in these areas? These will provide a clue to your purposes in life. List these purposes in order of importance to you.

Step Two. What beneficial personal characteristics do each of you contribute to these areas? One young woman may cite dedication, enthusiasm, and persistence as her important qualities, while another may feel her compassion, loyalty, and desire to learn are her dominant characteristics. What do you view as your most important attributes?

Step Three. Integrate the key purposes you both identified in Step One with the key personal characteristics you listed in Step Two. Ask each other for help in identifying your personal characteristics. If you are having trouble, refer back to your mirror talk or use the following list of characteristics:

Enthusiastic	Humorous	Optimistic
Compassionate	Grateful	Reasonable
Organized	Fair-minded	Reliable
Sincere	Kind	Friendly
Courageous	Adaptable	Strong
Conscientious	Growing	Resourceful
Forgiving	Thorough	Happy
Trustworthy	Loving	Intelligent
Patient	Adventurous	Creative
Generous	Competent	Determined
Wise	Assertive	Confident

Step Four. Write your personal mission statements. Include the important words and phrases you both noted in Step Three. Carry a rough draft with you and make notes, additions, and deletions, if you think of any changes. You probably will find that your first draft is not specific enough, or you may have left out something. For example, Rhonda found her first mission statement to be inadequate, too vague, so she revised it. Her original mission statement read, "Rhonda is a dedicated, enthusiastic young woman who strives for excellence in all her endeavors." By adding a few words, she improved it to better reflect who she is. Her mission statement then became, "Rhonda is a dedicated, enthusiastic young woman who strives for excellence in all her endeavors. She is committed to improving the quality of life for children and exemplifies kindness, understanding, and integrity."

Step Five. Each of you should memorize your mission statement and refer to it frequently. Use it as a standard by which you judge all your activities. Periodically review and evaluate your personal mission statement to determine if it continues to define who you are.

A mission statement clarifies things that you and your daughter otherwise might not know. Your daughter's mission statement is a way of discovering who she is and her sense of purpose in life. She is working to uncover the deepest and best within herself. Writing a personal mission statement is a quest of self-discovery.

WHERE ARE YOU GOING?

From *Alice in Wonderland* by Lewis Carroll.
Alice came to a fork in the road and saw a Cheshire Cat in a tree.
"Which road do I take?" she asked.
His response was a question: "Where do you want to go?"
"I don't know," Alice answered.
"Then," said the Cat, "it doesn't matter."

Your Vision: Who Do You Want to Become?

In 1946, Mother Teresa had a vision, a promise of mercy to spread love in the world by relieving poverty and sharing in the suffering of others. This passion led her in her calling to serve the poorest of the poor. Her work became a driving force that inspired the world. Selfless dedication to her vision continually gave Mother Teresa direction and focus.

Remaining faithful to her vision kept Mother Teresa from getting side-tracked with fame or fortune. Even after receiving the Nobel Peace Prize in 1979, she asked that the money for her celebration dinner be used to feed the poor. Her unerring commitment to her vision was evident throughout her life.

Vision is the second stage in developing a Lifetime Strategic Plan. It describes who you want to become, where you see yourself in the future, and what you want to accomplish. Vision is hope with a blueprint, a guide for all activities. Vision is not about wishful thinking. It requires action with a direction. Without direction, actions probably won't achieve the desired results. Vision with action changes lives. It can transform the world.

Pragmatic optimism is the current that gives energy to the vision. Author Winifred Newman once noted, "Vision is the world's most desperate need. There are no hopeless situations, only people who think hopelessly." Without the simple "I can" belief of optimism, visions are empty promises. If your daughter's vision is to feed the world and she believes she can do it, she will. The fuel of pragmatic optimism makes your daughter's vision an achievable and realistic goal.

Optimism fills vision with the potential for greatness. Like the gas tank in your car, the more fuel you have, the farther you can go. The more pragmatic optimism you have in your vision, the farther it will take you. The degree of belief and degree of action determine the level at which the vision can be realized. Although a vision may be simple, it is the extent to which you act upon it that allows it to be great.

For example, Rhonda's mission statement states, "Rhonda is a dedicated, enthusiastic young woman who strives for excellence in all her endeavors. She is committed to improving the quality of life for children and exemplifies kindness, understanding, and integrity." To form her vision, Rhonda looks at what she values in her mission statement and determines that children and their quality of life are extremely important to her. From this, she develops a vision that is in line with this mission. She defines her vision as "to develop a state-of-the-art recreational program that encourages children's self-reliance and dignity."

Tips from the Toolbox

You and your daughter can discover your visions by asking the right questions. Forget the petty or stressful situations you have going on at the moment and fast-forward through time to your grandchildren telling their children about you. What type of person do you hope they will describe? What do you want them to say about how you lived your life? How did you treat others? What was important to you? What do you hope they will describe as your legacy? Your vision is this hope.

Your Activity Plan: How Are You Going to Accomplish This?

Your daughter can have a dynamic mission statement and a passionate vision, but without an effective activity plan, she has nothing more than wishful thinking and empty promises. The third stage in Designing Your Lifetime Strategic Plan is to define the activity plan. An activity plan details specific actions necessary to accomplish outcomes that advance your daughter's personal mission statement and her vision. It tells what she wants to achieve, what she will do to accomplish this, and how she will measure its success.

For Rhonda to fulfill her mission of "improving the quality of life for children" and her vision of "a state-of-the-art recreational program that encourages children's self reliance and dignity," she will need action to back these words. As you look at this mission and vision, what are the key issues that will drive her program? What will be her priorities in developing an activity plan? Her program may require ten needed elements, but only three may be crucial. For instance, the children's safety, effective adult role models, and enjoyable activities may be more important than acquiring new equipment. These three elements will be her priorities in establishing her activity plan.

Now that Rhonda has established her three priorities, she can list measurable outcomes and required actions. In the realm of safety, she determines that the kids will be in a drug-free environment and safe from physical injury. Rhonda decides that she will ensure this by having a security guard on the premises, having structurally sound equipment, and enforcing a zero-tolerance policy for drugs.

In the evaluation of her activity plan, she will assess monthly the safety of the program by reviewing her records. She then can make the necessary changes that ensure the success of her plan. She will do this for each of her priorities, keeping in mind that they must be in line with her mission and vision.

Evaluation tends to be the most overlooked step in the activity plan. However, it may be the most important in keeping your daughter on track. Continuous feedback allows her to modify her plan as needed. An effective activity plan always allows for change and growth.

On the next page is a condensed version of Designing Your Lifetime Strategic Plan for your reference:

A MODEL OF THE LIFETIME STRATEGIC PLAN

Mission

A clear concise mission statement defines who you are and what
you do.
It has passion, humanity, and an eye for the big picture.
The purposes for your existence are found within your mission
statement.

Vision

Vision is where you see yourself in the future, and what you want to
accomplish.
Vision describes who you want to become.
Vision requires action with a direction.

Activity Plan

An activity plan details specific actions to accomplish outcomes.
It advances your mission and vision.
It includes specific actions, measurable outcomes, and timely
evaluation.

The Power Tool of Expanding Your Limits

"When one door of happiness closes, another opens; but often we look so long at the closed door that we do not see the one which has been opened for us."
— Helen Keller

It is human nature to walk in rutted pathways. You know the road's direction and where it will lead. Plodding down this familiar beaten path takes you to the same place every time. Its bumps and potholes, twists and turns are well known. It is usually the easier way because you know people have traveled it safely before. This tendency in human nature to follow the familiar path is similar to the journey of life. Many times, it is easier to follow the safe, sure route. But this easy path may not be the road to optimal fulfillment.

In the poem "The Road Not Taken," where "Two roads diverged in a wood, and I — I took the one less traveled by, and that has made all the difference," Robert Frost speaks of taking the road less traveled. In reality, the alternate path may not be visible or even exist. It may mean creating a road that others have not taken or even envisioned.

The world's greatest accomplishments would not exist if everyone traveled in well-worn, familiar footsteps. Great moments in history were made by men and women who forged new paths. Since the beginning of time, men and women have braved the wilderness, climbed mountains, crossed oceans, and launched into space. These adventurers shared a curiosity for the unknown, a desire for first experiences, the need to conquer challenges, and an excitement for the unexpected. The journey was not easy, and the method of transportation was often slow and treacherous. But for these pioneers, the outcome was worth the calculated risks. The push to expand known limits was responsible for great feats of heroism and discovery. Perhaps we would still be in caves if not for this courage.

Children are taught to conform to accepted patterns and norms. Most are taught to color within the lines, wear matching socks, and follow the leader.

They are often rescued from treetops and warned to play it safe. Young girls are especially vulnerable to this conditioning. Society reinforces views of women as model-thin peacemakers who never dare to question this stereotype. However, a pioneering spirit in each of us yearns to be uncovered. There is a push to expand known limits, though that push may be stifled or hidden.

Your daughter has an unlimited, untapped potential for greatness. She may not recognize her own adventurous nature, or her ability to expand her limits, but by digging up her drive and talents, she can unearth her potential. The power tool of Expanding Your Limits gives your daughter unlimited possibilities. It makes possible her visions and dreams. This power tool is essential not only for great adventurers, but for your daughter as well.

The power tool of Expanding Your Limits works best for your daughter when combined with the fuel of optimism. The "I can" attitude fuels this power tool with self-confidence. This "I can" belief provides her with a strong current to take charge and explore her boundaries. It allows her confidence to push the limits of these boundaries, knowing that she can handle new situations. Pragmatic optimism enables her to try new approaches, stay out of ruts, and seek more effective ways of achieving her goals. The power tool of Expanding Your Limits requires her to face new challenges, seize new opportunities, test her resources against the unknown, and in the process, discover her own unique potential. Expanding Your Limits with optimism takes a seemingly improbable goal and makes it a reality; it makes bold achievements possible and probable.

Your daughter must be willing to take calculated risks and step out of her comfort zone. Perhaps the greatest hazard in life is to risk nothing. A poem, "To Do Nothing," attributed to inspirational author and newspaper editor, William Arthur Ward clarifies this wisdom, "The person who risks nothing does nothing, has nothing, is nothing. He may avoid suffering and sorrow, but he cannot learn, feel change, grow or live. . . . He has forfeited his freedom. Only a person who risks is free." Your daughter can learn to expand her limits in dealing with the day-to-day obstacles of life. Even minor changes and difficulties can be resolved using this power tool fueled by optimism.

Tips from the Toolbox

Your daughter's Lifetime Strategic Plan is not set in stone. Not only should her plan change when goals and expectations change, but it should also be adjusted to fit opportunities. Opportunities for greatness do not often fall into your daughter's lap. Your daughter must actively seek them. Only by expanding her limits, pushing the envelope, and forging ahead can your daughter achieve her goals. Her journey begins with the first step.

The power tool of Expanding Your Limits is an attitude that relies on the Connected Inner Guide to calculate risks and hold fear captive. Expanding Your Limits does not mean attempting the truly impossible nor taking risks that are not worth the consequences. Some people have an unhealthy, misguided desire for danger. Expanding Your Limits is not about feeling an adrenaline high or heart-stopping thrill caused by unacceptable risks and danger. To expand her limits, your daughter must use her head to calculate the risks, her heart to assess the fear, and her gut to evaluate its value to her Lifetime Strategic Plan.

Often fear is a roadblock to Expanding Your Limits. If your daughter feels fear, she can view it as an indicator and calculate the danger. Fear is not the enemy. Expanding Your Limits lessens the fear of failure and the unknown because the familiarity of repeatedly trying something alleviates fear. Authors of *Focus on the Positive,* John Roger and Peter McWilliams, believe you need to try everything three times — first, to get over the fear; second, to find out how to do it; and third, to decide if you like it or not. When your daughter fears that she will not be successful in a new experience, she must rely on her Courageous Heart to redirect the fear and her Comforter to recall her vision in her Lifetime Strategic Plan. This will enable her to remove the paralyzing fear and put the gears in motion to accomplish her goal.

When your daughter envisions her dream and imagines herself at the peak of its realization, she affirms and clarifies her dream to expand her limits. By luxuriating in its glory and imagining its pitfalls, she is better equipped to assess her aspiration. The following questions can help her expand her limits to realize her dreams:

- Are you afraid? If you are afraid, what does your Courageous Heart tell you is causing your fear? Is it real danger or is it the fear of the unknown?
- What are the associated risks? Let your head's Comforter calculate the risks involved. Are the risks real or are they distorted perceptions of the Toxic Inner Critic?
- How does your dream fit with your Lifetime Strategic Plan?
- Is your dream in line with the values of your Trained Conscience?

Once your daughter answers these questions, her Connected Inner Guide can weigh the risk versus the potential outcome and make a decision. When your daughter expands her limits within her Lifetime Strategic Plan, this helps her feel both physically and emotionally safe.

Trying teaches what is easy to do, what is hard to do, and what is impossible. Self-confidence is achieved by testing and expanding your limits. The more your daughter tries and learns that she can, the more she will be willing to try. Self-worth escalates as she expands her limits. She expands exponentially each time she ventures into new territory.

 Tips from the Toolbox

The first step for your daughter to expand her limits is to be willing to forge ahead. She must be willing to go where others may not have gone. She must blaze a new trail, make mistakes, start over. She just needs to keep plugging away. It's the true secret of success. The law of averages says she won't fail every time, and the only true failure is the failure to try.

Managing Difficult Tasks

Inevitably in life, there are certain things your daughter is required to do that she doesn't do well. Because she does not do these tasks well, she may not want to do them. This does not mean she should not do them. Winners do what losers do not want to do. Sometimes, it is necessary that your daughter do what she does not want to do. It may be a necessary path for reaching her goals, it may teach valuable lessons and it may offer an unexpected opportunity.

Undesirable tasks can affect your daughter physically and psychologically. Performing difficult tasks can make her anxious, irritable, overwhelmed, or even ambivalent. She might procrastinate or totally ignore the job. She might become overly perfectionistic or perform ineffectively. Even thinking about the overwhelming task can make her nauseous.

Although your daughter must occasionally do difficult tasks, she does not have to suffer. Before you see her struggling, you can teach your daughter several ways she can manage her weaknesses. Depending on the task, one or more tricks of management can assist her in getting the job done.

If the job is large, break the task down. Breaking down a seemingly impossible task into smaller steps helps get a gigantic job done. An old joke asks: "How do you eat an elephant?" Answer: "One bite at a time." It is through perseverance and simply taking one step at a time that your daughter can accomplish the almost impossible.

After reducing the task into smaller, manageable tasks, celebrate each accomplishment along the way. A little recognition or reward for each small accomplishment goes a long way to increase your daughter's motivation.

Do the hard stuff first. As Norman Vincent Peale instructed, "Don't duck the most difficult problems. That just insures that the hardest part will be left when you're most tired. Get the big one done — it's downhill from then on."

Get help if you need it. Your daughter needs to know that asking for help is not a sign of weakness. Not only can asking for help give the needed answers, but it can generate support from the person she asks.

Do not let perfectionism keep you from participating. In activities that your daughter does not do well, having to do her best can prevent her from doing something she might enjoy. In these cases, doing is more important than being the best.

Don't procrastinate. Create a deadline. This might motivate your daughter to get the job finished. When she gives in to procrastination, she is giving in to uncertainty and self-doubt. "Not now" many times becomes "not ever."

Is the task a necessary step toward achieving a goal? If it is not and can be omitted, your daughter should do so. Daniel Webster once noted, "There is nothing so wasteful as doing with great efficiency that which doesn't have to be done at all."

If the task doesn't require it, don't spend hours striving for perfection. Your daughter should target some areas in her Lifetime Strategic Plan in which she will do her best. In others, she can be satisfied with simply getting the job done.

In reaching for goals, your daughter will find what does and does not work for her, and consequently, discover her strengths and weaknesses. Once she recognizes her strengths and weaknesses, she can work on a plan to make each work for her rather than against her. The only way she can determine her strengths is by trying. The only way to know her limits is to go beyond them.

Everyone has a pioneering spirit waiting to be uncovered. The power tool of Expanding Your Limits offers unlimited possibilities and teaches your daughter that she can. Fueled with optimism, this power tool can drive her "to boldly go where no one has gone before." Expanding Your Limits requires your daughter to embrace new challenges, test personal resources against the unknown, and in the process, discover her own unique potential.

The Power Tool of Experiencing the Humor

"The human race has only one really effective weapon, and that's laughter. The moment it arises, all our hardnesses yield, all our irritations and resentments slip away, and a sunny spirit takes their place." — Mark Twain

Some cultures believe you are not a social being until you laugh. In the Navajo Indian culture, the importance of laughter is shown by the First Laugh Ceremony. Tradition dictates that a baby is kept in the cradle board until she laughs for the first time. This means that others continually watch until the laugh occurs. This laugh signifies her birth as a social being. The person who witnesses the first laugh performs a First Laugh Ceremony to honor the child's first laugh and her emergence as a social being. The Navajo Indians understand the power of laughter and humor.

Humor is a powerful technique for social, psychological, and physical growth. The power tool of Experiencing the Humor promotes self-transformation and self-worth. Fueled by pragmatic optimism, humor enables people to feel a sense of self-protection and control in their environment. Humor gives people a perceptual flexibility that increases their cognitive control in situations. Sociologist and author S. C. Kobassa believes that while you cannot control the external world, you can control how you view events and the emotional responses you choose.

Jessica, a fourteen-year-old aspiring actor, tells how humor lent cognitive control in a situation she recently faced. On opening night at the school play, Jessica had an important scene in which she delivered a lengthy monologue. She was mortified because she missed a few lines. Afterward, her drama teacher comforted her by saying that nobody noticed, but her best friend, Christopher, teased her about the mistake.

Jessica was relieved to realize she had a choice — she could be negative or she could be positive. She could listen to her Crybaby Heart scream, "How humiliating!" and her Toxic Inner Critic snarl, "You are so stupid." Her Crybaby Heart's negative reaction, amplified by the Toxic Inner Critic, could have magnified the hurt and humiliation. But Jessica permitted her Courageous Heart and Comforter to join forces and help her put events into perspective. Her Courageous Heart silenced her Crybaby Heart by saying, "Quit feeling sorry for yourself. Don't be embarrassed. It was kind of funny." Her Comforter defeated her Toxic Inner Critic by reasoning, "This is not such a big deal. Your poise and delivery showed the hard work you put into this part. One day you may laugh about this." Several weeks later, as she recounted the story, she could see the humor in the situation and actually laughed about it.

In this example, Jessica's head and heart made a conscious choice to protect her and use the power tool of humor. Using humor, Jessica was later able to laugh with Christopher and say, "Yeah, Shakespeare probably rolled over in his grave last night." Jessica allowed humor to take away the sting of her embarrassment and help her to feel better about herself. The power tool of Experiencing the Humor empowered her to build a stronghold that could withstand the attacks of her Toxic Inner Critic and Crybaby Heart.

Because of its tension-alleviating effects, humor is an effective antidote for the Toxic Inner Critic's distortions of self-righteous, all-or-nothing thinking. A sense of humor can bring dogmatic thinking into perspective. You probably know people who are sure they have the only answer and anything else is wrong. If you oppose them, they might imply that you are foolish and out of line. By humorously looking at the absurdity of their thoughts, you can alleviate this tension. Humor helps put events into perspective.

There may be times when your daughter is unwilling to compromise or see another's viewpoint. By stepping away from rigid thinking and admitting that others really aren't that stupid, your daughter can create a starting place for humor. The real issue in self-righteous thinking is power and control, and she gains cognitive control when she can use the power tool of humor.

It is important not to view teasing and hurtful laughter as humor. Healthy humor cannot coexist with negative emotions. Real humor is not at the expense of another person's feelings and doesn't make fun of another's disappointments or inadequacies. Laughing at rather than with brings about negative emotions and defeats the healing goodness of humor.

In a world that is not always fair, Experiencing the Humor, charged by pragmatic optimism, is a tool that can break the incongruities in life and allow your daughter to perceive the world in a more realistic way. If she unrealistically views the world as fair, she may be angry when it does not treat her fairly. Her lack of control in an unfair situation creates anger that feeds her stress. Humor allows her to assume a certain amount of control. As Ann Richards, the former governor of Texas once commented, "Humor is a lifesaver for me. If I can't see the amusement and the silliness of the human condition in everything I do, I lose my perspective." When your daughter views her stress using humor and pragmatic optimism, she controls its damage.

Tips from the Toolbox

Many are familiar with the phrase "It wasn't funny at the time."
Help your daughter realize that time often provides an alternate

perspective. Find the humor in embarrassing situations that once caused pain. Let go of the past. They say angels can fly because they take themselves lightly. Lighten up!

Healing Humor

In today's fast-paced, competitive world, tension and stress have become the norm rather than the exception. This is true not only for adults but for all age groups. A preschooler can be involved in so many activities that she starts her day tired and cranky. A grade schooler might wake up with stomachaches and nausea. A teen may procrastinate over term papers or drag her feet getting ready in the morning. Each age group faces its own stressors. Tension, fatigue, and hopelessness are the by-products of a fast-paced lifestyle that demands perfection.

The power tool of Experiencing the Humor can give your daughter the ability to feel joy and release tension. As she experiences stress, the physical and emotional immune systems use antibodies to help cope. These antibodies must be regenerated to prevent the body from becoming susceptible to toxins. Humor regenerates these needed antibodies. Patty Wooten, R.N. and humor expert, notes in her article "Humor: An Antidote for Stress," that research has proven that biochemically, humor increases immunoglobulin A and decreases the stress hormones. Also, these humor-induced antibodies can be stockpiled and used as needed. Because of humor's immediate positive effects on the immune system and its long-term ability to increase the storage of antibodies, it is a healing power tool. Humor can change your daughter's biochemistry to help her cope with stress and boost her immune system.

Laughter, humor's by-product, has important health benefits, as well. Like exercise, it increases relaxation. Research shows that one hundred to two hundred deep chuckles benefit the body as much as ten minutes of rowing. Laughter lowers the blood pressure, exercises the lungs, and stimulates the circulatory system. It also has been shown to increase the body's endorphins or natural painkillers. The reason behind the laugh may also distract from the pain. Laughter is a good workout. Laugh for good health.

A good start for incorporating the power tool of Experiencing the Humor is to smile. A smile has been shown to do more than make you look good. Two of the key facial muscles used to smile trigger the same change in brain activity that occur when you are naturally happy. If your daughter's Crybaby Heart is angry or unhappy, perhaps she should smile. This will send a signal of happiness to the brain. This mind-body connection can be the first step toward experiencing humor.

Experiencing the Humor is an extremely useful tool, but how can your daughter learn to develop it? Using the following suggestions, your daughter can learn to incorporate humor into her daily activities.

Find joy and humor in simple matters. Your daughter can look for the joy and humor in everyday life. When she stays in touch with her playful inner nature, she can recapture her sense of wonder. If she has neglected this, she can rekindle her sense of awe. When she doesn't take herself too seriously, she can find joy and humor in simple matters.

Welcome change. The best way to find humor in new situations is to alter personal views on change. Humor, when coupled with the power tool of Expanding Your Limits, can alleviate your daughter's fear and allow her to find control and be proactive. Humor can help her embrace change as movement forward.

Lighten up. When your daughter learns to laugh at herself, she can view her mistakes more easily as learning experiences. She needs to be compassionate, love herself, and feel free to laugh at herself and with others.

Collect humor. Your daughter might enjoy writing down the funny episodes in her life. Joke books, movies, cartoons, and songs all offer sources for humor. As she collects humor, she should keep these handy for the times she needs a smile. She can place her favorites on her mirror, bulletin board, or in her purse. She can share them with others. When she experiences humor, she can encourage others to smile and laugh with her.

Life may not always treat your daughter fairly and it is certainly not always logical, but life's changes can be less stressful when humor is employed. She can hasten healing, both physically and emotionally, through its use. Humor, energized by pragmatic optimism, brings an "I can" perspective that promotes

a sense of control that is vital to health and self-worth. Even in extreme circumstances, she can regain a sense of control through the power tool of
Experiencing the Humor.

The Power Tool of Gratitude:
Unearthing Hidden Treasures

----

*"How wonderful it would be if we could help our children and grandchildren to
learn thanksgiving at an early age. Thanksgiving opens the doors. It changes a
child's personality. A child is resentful, negative — or thankful. Thankful children
want to give, they radiate happiness, they draw people"*
— Sir John Marks Templeton

The English word *thanks* comes from the same Anglo-Saxon word as *think*.
Thinking is an active process that involves reflection and conscious
awareness. The power tool of Gratitude or giving thanks requires this same
conscious awareness and reflection. When your daughter becomes aware of
the many endowments she has been given in life, indifference to her situation
is impossible. She must make a conscious choice of how to respond — with
gratitude or ingratitude.

Because she cannot possibly take in all the stimuli that bombard her every
moment, your daughter may slip into an automatic pilot mode. The push and
crush of everyday life generates stress that can force her into a zombie-like
existence. Her busyness leaves little time for awareness. Awareness may seem
like another task to add to an already hectic schedule, but it can initiate
gratitude. Awareness gives your daughter the choice to be grateful or not and
opens the door to the power tool of Gratitude, which can help unearth many
concealed treasures in your daughter's life.

A lack of awareness steals the right to experience the power tool of
Gratitude. Some people are neither grateful nor ungrateful. This condition
of indifference exists in people who are unaware and do not assess their

blessings and struggles. Indifference can be cured by awareness. When your daughter becomes aware, indifference is impossible. Assuming your daughter is not sleeping through life in apathy, if she is not grateful for what she has been given, she is ungrateful.

Tips from the Toolbox

One way your daughter can explore her wealth of hidden gifts is to look back to her Lifetime Strategic Plan in Step Two of her mission statement. What were the personal attributes she listed? Now, have a friend list ten qualities they appreciate in her. As she keeps adding to her list, she can choose to be grateful for the person she is. She should appreciate her strengths and find a gentle acceptance of her imperfections. This can help her become aware of who she is and be grateful.

Gratitude — Not *Just an Attitude*

The power tool of Gratitude is especially effective when fueled with pragmatic optimism. Dr. Max More observes that being proactive, coupled with a strong sense of abundance, creates personal energy. Grateful people recognize that the world is full of opportunities. They are for things, not against them and proactive, not reactive. When your daughter is proactive, she focuses on changing the bad. She creates alternatives, excites others about new options, and feels productive and creative.

Optimism generates gratitude. Gratitude is an activity that increases enthusiasm. This leads to effort and progress, which validate gratitude and generate more optimism, which creates more gratitude. A circle of gratitude occurs. William Faulkner once noted that gratitude is a quality similar to electricity: It must be produced, discharged, and used up to exist at all. Gratitude is not just an attitude. Gratitude is an activity.

Not only is gratitude a thinking "I can" attitude, but it is a "doing" activity. In *I Heard the Owl Call My Name,* author Margaret Craven tells of a young clergyman sent to a remote parish among the Kwakiutl Indians in British

Columbia. The young minister discovers that the Indians do not have a word for *thank you,* but they have an exceptional generosity. Instead of saying thanks, they customarily return every kindness with an equal or superior kindness. They do rather than speak their thanks.

Gratitude — Not an Entitlement

Gratitude is often pushed into the background of American thought. In the modern fast-paced world, it is easy to overlook the gifts in life. Today's generation seems to feel the world owes them. Many feel it is their right to realize the American Dream regardless of their effort, or lack of effort. In his article "Gratitude at the Soup Line," Dennis Dillon recounts a story he heard on the radio while traveling the open spaces of West Texas. The radio talk-show host was discussing the American economy. One caller on the show asked, "If we experienced another great depression, what would be the difference from the first one?" The reply was, "There would be no gratitude at the soup line."

This lack of gratitude at the soup line exemplifies an attitude of entitlement that fails to appreciate the value of hard work. It is not necessarily the outcome of the labor that gives gratification, but the amount of time and energy invested that generates this gratitude. When your daughter works hard for something, her accomplishment tastes sweeter and this enables appreciation. When she views her bounty as her prerogative, she forfeits her power tool of Gratitude.

Gratitude — A Matter of Focus

Ingratitude is a destructive force that ruins not only society, but individuals and their families. A common mistake made in relationships is to lose gratitude because of a negative focus. Taking things for granted and narrowing in on the negatives can rob parents of the joys of a sound relationship with their daughters. Jim and Theresa are prime examples of parents who love their daughter dearly, but fail to appreciate her good qualities. While their intentions initially were good, their failure to see their daughter in a positive light created a painful battle. Their daughter, Katie, had a few habits that frustrated Jim and Theresa. They thought that if Katie just changed a few habits, she would be the ideal person. They wanted her to be that person for her own sake. At first, they encouraged her to change these habits, then they insisted, then they demanded, and finally, they threatened. This infuriated Katie; she shut down and became alienated from her parents. Even though Katie had many admirable qualities, Jim and Theresa chose to focus on her irritating habits. Because they failed to acknowledge her many good qualities, because they focused only on the habits that frustrated them, they lost touch with Katie. If Jim and Theresa had maintained an optimistic perspective, and focused on more of Katie's positive attributes and fewer of her annoying traits, they could have maintained their communicative relationship.

Just as Jim and Theresa lost their optimistic perspective, many people choose their focus unwisely. Things that irritate you about others may be insignificant when compared to the things that you value and appreciate in them. An awareness and recognition of others' good qualities are vital to healthy relationships.

 Tips from the Toolbox

Like Jim and Theresa, who failed to recognize their daughter's good points, you can fall into the trap of not appreciating your loved ones for who they are. If you postpone being grateful until they are perfect, you will miss a gift not only for them but also for yourself. Find something positive to appreciate and say it to the people you care about every day.

Gratitude — Not Circumstance Dependent

If your daughter makes gratitude circumstance dependent, it will take her much longer to have what she desires to create the joy, love, and happiness she seeks. She will be constantly searching for an elusive want, rather than appreciating the joy, love, and happiness that she already has.

It is easy to be grateful when things are going well, but what about being grateful for the bad? Your daughter may not realize that she can be upset and grateful at the same time. What happens in her life is not always in her control, but she does control her awareness and the choice to be grateful. She can choose to be consumed by the distress of the immediate, or she can choose to become more aware of the good in her life. This is an important choice. Whatever your daughter focuses on expands. If she chooses to be consumed with her distress and lives in discontentment, even life's best situations will be filled with gloom and depression. If she chooses to remember her blessings, she will be able to live in gratitude even when she is distressed. Then, in life's worst situations, she will find light instead of darkness, hope instead of despair.

Gratitude may not be instantaneous in distressful situations, but it can be achieved over time with the help of an optimistic "I can" attitude. Your daughter can empower herself to maneuver through tough situations by saying, "I can handle whatever comes along." The power tool of Gratitude fueled with optimism enables her to move forward in difficult times. Gratitude is a gift she gives herself.

The Buddhist book *Anguttara Nikaya* states, "The unworthy man is ungrateful, forgetful of benefits [done to him]. This ingratitude, this forgetfulness is congenial to mean people. . . . But the worthy person is grateful and mindful of benefits done to him. This gratitude, this mindfulness, is congenial to the best people." Awareness coupled with gratitude allows your daughter to count herself among worthy people.

Appreciation of true worth is a turning point in your daughter's finding her self-worth. The key lies in the power tool of Gratitude. Through gratitude and awareness, your daughter counts herself among the best and the valued, and therefore, worthy of her own regard. When she is satisfied with who she is at any given time, she has self-worth.

The act of being grateful gives your daughter more than just gratitude. By employing the power tool of Gratitude, your daughter gains awareness, optimism, appreciation, and self-worth. The power tool of Gratitude always blesses the grateful.

The Power Tool of Cultivating Unconditional Love

"The greatest disease in the West today is not TB or leprosy; it is being unwanted, unloved, and uncared for." — Mother Teresa

Unconditional love is psychological nourishment for a human being. Unconditional love stands alone. It is independent of words, actions, prejudices, and perfectionism. True unconditional love is present regardless of circumstances. It is absolute in its nature. To be loved unconditionally is to realize that you are worthy of respect and are valued just as you are.

Loving and being loved unconditionally is a cornerstone in building self-worth. Author and addiction recovery counselor Pia Mellody (as quoted in *The Miracle of Change* by Dennis Wholey) states, "The most important thing children need to learn is that they are absolutely good enough in spite of the fact they are imperfect. Self-love is the single most powerful lesson a child will ever learn." Unconditional love of self forms a mighty core of self-esteem.

Cultivating unconditional love is one of the Connected Inner Guide's most powerful tools in making decisions. It disarms the Toxic Inner Critic, quiets the Crybaby Heart, and defeats the Creep. Empowering the Connected Inner Guide with unconditional love enables the Comforter to stand on solid reasoning, the Courageous Heart to lean on healthy emotions, and the Trained Conscience to aspire to its highest principles. Unconditional self-love conquers negativity and brings out the best of the Connected Inner Guide.

There are two aspects to the power tool of Cultivating Unconditional Love — unconditional love of self and unconditional love of others. Of these two aspects, unconditional love of self must come first. Pia Mellody supports this point by stating, "Love starts with the thought: I am enough. I matter, in spite of the fact that I am imperfect." When your daughter makes the choice to love herself, flaws and all, she becomes aware of her innate worthiness. Having imperfections makes her real. Accepting these imperfections as necessary is vital to her unconditional love. Unconditional love of self is the awareness that she should be loved just as she is.

Dr. Wayne Dyer, in his book *Your Erroneous Zones,* notes that to receive unconditional love, your daughter must feel worthy of it. If she is unable to love herself, then giving becomes impossible. How can she give love if she is worthless? What would her love be worth? And if she can't give love, she can't receive it. The power tool of Cultivating Unconditional Love for your daughter starts with loving herself.

Cultivating unconditional love is not a nebulous concept. There are specific defining elements that unconditional love encompasses. According to Stephen Covey in *The Seven Habits of Highly Effective Families,* three primary laws govern unconditional love:

- Acceptance rather than rejection
- Understanding rather than judgment
- Participation rather than manipulation

"Practicing unconditional love is a proactive choice that is not based on another's behavior or on social status, educational attainment, wealth, reputation, or any other factor except the intrinsic worth of a human being," states Covey. When your daughter loves without the expectation of anything coming back to her in return, this is unconditional love. It is love without conditions or qualifications. It is given without reservations or prerequisites. It is not earned or deserved, it just is.

Your daughter should avoid falling into the trap of conditional love. Covey defines conditional love as the love of the outcome rather than the person. When your daughter makes a decision to withhold her love based on what she wants to happen, she is rejecting or manipulating that person by judging what is worthy of her love. This sends the message that her love is only available when the other person pleases her.

By making the decision to cultivate unconditional love, your daughter does not necessarily condone others' weaknesses or agree with their opinions; she simply affirms others' intrinsic worth.

- Conditional love tears down.
- Conditional love dislikes, magnifies faults, and destroys confidence and competence.

- Conditional love undermines others' worth with criticism and negative remarks or gestures.
- Conditional love's goal is to manipulate and control.

- Unconditional love builds up.
- Unconditional love is supportive, accepts, and loves.

- Unconditional love is always loyal to others.

- Unconditional love believes in others' worth and potential.

Your love for your daughter should not be contingent on her conforming to your expectations. In *Your Erroneous Zones,* Dr. Dyer further defines unconditional love of others as the actions that allow those that you care for to be what they choose for themselves, without any insistence that they satisfy you. (For more help with learning to cultivate unconditional love with your daughter, refer to the section in chapter 1 titled "The Good, the Bad, and the Ugly: Loving Her No Matter What" on page 10.)

Cultivating Unconditional Love

Unconditional love is easier to define than to cultivate. The power tool of Cultivating Unconditional Love requires patience and work, much like a well-kept garden does. Your daughter must tend it carefully and continuously long before it bears fruit. Just as the gardener must cultivate the soil, prepare the land, plant the crop, weed and feed the plants, and wait for the harvest, she must spend much time and effort cultivating unconditional love before she sees the results. Even though the results of unconditional love may not be readily apparent, she must have confidence that eventually the fruit will ripen and her careful cultivation will produce results. Like the gardener, it helps to have some tools in her basket to help in this endeavor.

How can your daughter develop these tools? How can she stop insisting others satisfy her wants? How can she allow others to be their own person? How can she cultivate unconditional love?

Your daughter must love herself. Unconditional love starts with loving her own uniqueness and being secure. Your daughter should avoid listening to the negative voice that says she doesn't deserve it or isn't good enough. She should value her feelings and not violate her principles and values. Simply put, your daughter can love herself unconditionally by listening to her healthy Connected Inner Guide.

Your daughter should accept others as they are. She should neither want nor need them to be like her. That would rob them of their uniqueness, the traits that make them special and separate.

Your daughter should learn to listen empathetically, without making judgments. Walking in another's shoes for a brief time may give your daughter compassion and new insights. Remember, active listening makes others feel valued.

Your daughter can share her feelings and opinions. This allows others to know her better and to feel valued and included.

Her conversations should avoid criticism. When something goes wrong, self-evaluation and exploring options without harsh judgment form the answer to building unconditional love.

Another way your daughter can develop the tool of unconditional love is to **view others' actions compassionately and show kindness.** It is beneficial for her to make praise a part of her communication with others. Effective compliments should be specific, genuinely praising both performance and personal characteristics. A kind word or a pat on the back goes a long way.

The power tool of Cultivating Unconditional Love runs on the fuel of optimism. Your daughter must have faith that everything will work out and trust in her own potential and that of others. To be loved unconditionally, she must appreciate that she is worthy of love and respect just as she is. For her to give love unconditionally, she must appreciate the same worth in others.

This innate worthiness, this unconditional love, is the caretaker of self-worth. The power tool of Cultivating Unconditional Love creates a protective environment in which self-esteem grows and flourishes. It cultivates the soil with its faith and trust, it weeds out doubt and guilt, and it nourishes self-esteem with its unqualified acceptance and support.

Self-worth is rooted in unconditional acceptance of self, regardless of mistakes. There is a poem called "After a While" that depicts the path to self-esteem.

> After a while you learn the subtle difference between holding a
>> hand and chaining a soul.
> And you learn that love doesn't mean leaning and company
>> doesn't always mean security.
> And you begin to learn that kisses aren't contracts and presents
>> aren't promises.
> And you begin to accept your defeats with your head up and your
>> eyes ahead
>> with the grace of a woman, not the grief of a child.
> And you learn to build all your roads on today because
>> tomorrow's ground is
>> too uncertain for plans and futures have a way of falling
>> down in mid-flight.
> After a while you learn that even sunshine burns if you get too
>> much.
> So you plant your own garden and decorate your own soul
>> instead of waiting for someone to bring you flowers.
> And you learn that you really can endure
>> you really are strong
>> you really do have worth
> And you learn and you learn, with every goodbye, you learn...

© 1971 by Veronica A. Shoffstall

Tips from the Toolbox

Practically speaking, self-love often begins with merely treating yourself better. When your daughter treats herself as someone she truly cherishes, self-love invariably happens. By soothing herself when she is upset, avoiding foolish mistakes, and forgiving herself when she errs, she can comfortably bask in self-love.

The Power Tool of Resting in Spirituality

"Ask where the good way is, and walk in it, and you will find rest for your souls."
— Jeremiah 6:16

Have you ever laughed so hard that it brought tears to your eyes? Has the depth or richness of nature ever filled you with deep appreciation and awareness? Have you ever been touched by the unqualified love of a child? Is there a song that swells your heart with emotion? When you experience these moments of awareness, you are operating from your spiritual self. The spiritual self is that place deep within — an oasis of peace, joy, power, love, healing, and wisdom.

Since the very beginning of time, spirituality has permeated the hearts of man. Its existence has been recognized throughout the world. Although it may be called by different names in different parts of the world, spirituality has a universal underlying theme. Spirituality invokes a power greater than ourselves that calls us beyond ourselves.

In its simplest form, spirituality states, "Because I was created by God, I am a child of his. Because I am a child of God, I am worthy. Because I am worthy, I have value." Because your daughter is a spiritual being, she has great worth and purpose.

So, how can your daughter get in touch with her spirituality? According to minister and author Amy Taylor, all you need to do to find spirituality is "turn to the very center of your being, asking God's Presence and Power. Enter the Silence and the stillness, focusing your mind upon God, the Omnipotent good. Surrender to your Oneness and your consciousness will be carried to the realm of the Infinite, beyond words and thoughts, beyond time and space, into the Truth in which you live and move and have your being."

To find rest in spirituality, she goes on to say, "You need not try to still your mind. To do so is resistance and you need resist nothing. Simply turn within knowing that as you seek you will find that Something greater than yourself enlivening you, infilling you with a certainty, a substance that is so much more than what you know yourself to be."

Once your daughter knows how to tap into her spirituality, how can she actually rest in this spirituality? The power tool of Resting in Spirituality is a "being" rather than a "doing" power tool. Your daughter does not have to create anything. She does not have to invent this inner wealth because it is already there. She only has to acknowledge and call upon it. Resting in spirituality simply requires that your daughter be at peace in accepting that there is an omniscient Higher Power at work in her life. There is a medieval Jewish poem that offers a blessing for resting in spirituality:

> May you lie down in peace my friend,
> May you rise up full of wonder.
> Wrap yourself in the One
> morning after morning,
> O refresh your weary soul,
> Your only one, perfect and pure.
> If you do not keep your own soul alive,
> How will you welcome the morning light?
> How will you welcome the morning?
> Listen to the One,
> the song of the morning stars,
> Let the One open your heart.

The voice of God is always present. All your daughter needs to do is call upon it. Once she has invited the presence of the Higher Power, she can begin to experience the ultimate and purest form of unconditional love. By deciding to remember in faith that God is always with her, your daughter can experience the peace of resting in spirituality.

The power tool of Resting in Spirituality is your daughter's cornerstone of strength that her Connected Inner Guide rests upon as it makes decisions. In your daughter's healthy Connected Inner Guide, her Comforter, Courageous Heart, and Trained Conscience can rely on her Higher Power for strength, direction, and guidance. Feeling, thinking, and acting in accordance with her foundation of spirituality generates a sense of meaning and overriding purpose that powerfully impacts your daughter's daily decisions.

Making decisions relying on her spirituality will allow your daughter to experience an unparalleled richness in her life. Resting in spirituality provides her with unconditional love, joy, hope, faith, healing, forgiveness, freedom from fear, and abounding miracles.

Without belief, your daughter suffers from what Dr. Roberto Assagioli, the founder of psychosynthesis, calls "divine homesickness." Your daughter's divine homesickness leaves her lonely, lost, and empty. Her alienation and confusion prevent her Connected Inner Guide from functioning as her healthy decision-making tool. When your daughter finds her Higher Power, she can operate with a centered, abundant sense of confidence and peace.

Your daughter must develop her spiritual self to become aware of the miracles in her life. Below are some of the ways Dr. Wayne Dyer, in his book *Real Magic*, contrasts spiritual people with nonspiritual people:

The Nonspiritual Being	The Spiritual Being
■ is motivated by achievement, performance, and acquisitions	■ is motivated by ethics, serenity, and quality of life
■ lives exclusively within the five senses	■ realizes that there is more in life than the physical
■ believes we are alone in the universe	■ knows we are never alone
■ is focused on external power	■ is focused on personal empowerment
■ feels separated from all others	■ feels connected with all others
■ believes exclusively in cause and effect	■ knows there is a higher power at work
■ dismisses internal guidance as a hunch	■ believes in divine guidance or God talking
■ has no sense of responsibility to the universe	■ has a reverence for life
■ is laden with hostility, grudges, and revenge	■ understands the importance of forgiveness

The power tool of Resting in Spirituality is the only "being" power tool, unlike the "doing" nature of the other six tools. Adjusting Your Mirror, Expanding Your Limits, and Designing Your Lifetime Strategic Plan are all examples of tools that require deliberate action. Cultivating Unconditional

Love, Experiencing the Humor, and Gratitude require a conscious response. Resting in Spirituality, though, is a peaceful, abundant refuge for your daughter, a resting place for the weary doer. Spirituality always was, is, and will be.

Tips from the Toolbox

If your daughter experiences feelings of emptiness or intense loneliness, this may be a clue that she is not resting in her spirituality. From time to time, her well of spirituality may seem dry and require a little priming. The water is always there, but it just needs a boost. Prompting the flow with a little water may bring forth an abundant supply. You can give her a place to start by showing her how you find meaning and strength from resting in your spirituality.

A Toolbox for Your Daughter

---

*"We shall not fail or falter; we shall not weaken or tire....
Give us the tools and we will finish the job."* — Sir Winston S. Churchill

As your daughter begins making decisions with her Connected Inner Guide and maximizes the power tools fueled by pragmatic optimism, her toolbox can help her build a life of abundance, joy, peace, and purpose. These tools help her realize a zest for life that enables her to experience the fullness and excitement of a gratifying existence. The hammer in her hand coupled with these seven extremely powerful tools can assist your daughter in building a fortress of strength and self-worth and navigating skillfully through life's storms.

The hammer, the Connected Inner Guide, can strengthen and improve her decision-making skills, and the seven power tools can enhance the quality of your daughter's life in many practical ways. She visualizes the best she can be through mirror talk when she adjusts her mirror. She creates and implements a plan for her life when she designs her Lifetime Strategic Plan. She calculates her strengths and weaknesses, and forges ahead when she expands her limits. She lets humor heal her physically and emotionally when she uses the power tool of Experiencing the Humor. She unearths the hidden treasures of gratitude and awareness when she employs gratitude. She forms a culture of unconditional love for herself and others when she cultivates unconditional love. She listens to her soul when she rests in spirituality.

While your daughter can use these tools without added power, they are more effective when she plugs into the current of optimism. The "I can" attitude of optimism is not only the force that charges the power tools but may be the master key to unlock your daughter's strength and self-worth.

These power tools are effective individually but are even more effective when they are combined. Your daughter can combine the power tools to better handle everyday situations. For instance, your daughter might decide to apply for a part-time job at the mall. Due to traffic, she is late for the interview, and they have already filled the position. She may use her power tool of adjusting her mirror after this rejection to view herself more positively. She can go one step further and harness the electrical force of optimism. By believing that she has other opportunities, she can come up with a new plan. The new plan could lead her to expand her limits by applying for a different type of job while she is at the mall. These tools joined together equip your daughter with powerful life skills to deal with daily stresses.

Your daughter faces overwhelming challenges, unknown to previous generations. For her to live her life to the fullest, she surely needs a toolbox fitted with the hammer of decision-making, a strong Connected Inner Guide, and the seven power tools fueled with optimism. Her toolbox equips your daughter with the tools to build and restructure her life to make better decisions and to reach her fullest potential. As you help your daughter acquire these tools, she can customize her toolbox to handle any situation no matter how difficult.

Like the builder, your daughter can become more proficient with the tools the more she uses them. The more she uses them, the more your daughter learns that she can count on them. Then in difficult times, she will have her tools honed and ready for use when she needs them the most.

In addition to practicing the use of these tools to derive the most benefit from them, your daughter will need to learn some techniques to keep her toolbox itself in working order. In the next chapter, we will examine how she can keep her toolbox in good shape to maximize its effectiveness.

HONING THE SKILLS
What You Can Do

Prioritizing Spirituality in Your Life — *This exercise offers you a perspective on how well you rest in your spirituality.*

Take time out each day to develop your own spirituality. Pray, read spiritual material, meditate, and so on. Model your spirituality and allow your daughter to develop hers.

What You Can Do with Your Older Daughter (Ages Thirteen to Twenty-Three)

Designing Your Lifetime Strategic Plan — *This discussion will convey the importance of having a plan of action to achieve goals.*

Sit down with your daughter and perhaps your entire family and talk about the Lifetime Strategic Plan and the difference it can make in your lives. You may want to use the chart on page 153 to help you in your discussion.

Incorporating Humor — *This awareness can help your daughter benefit from humor.*

Humor can be learned. To find new ways to increase this skill, your daughter will find it helpful to be around people who exhibit humor. Does she associate with optimistic people that have a sense of humor? If not, discuss with her who can she bring into her life that has this quality. She can learn from them and benefit from the humor they exhibit.

What You Can Do with Your Younger Daughter (Ages Six to Twelve)

Playing the Fortress Word Game — *This fun exercise helps your daughter understand the aspects of her inner fortress, the place inside where she can stand self-assured and where she can replenish herself.*

> Write the word fortress at the top of a sheet of notebook paper. Together, you and your daughter think of as many words as you can that contain the root word fort. Some examples are fortitude, comfort, effort. How many more can you think of?

Finding Practical Ways to Rest in Spirituality — *This activity will help promote contemplative time for your daughter.*

> Help your daughter collect some fun things to place in a "Peace and Quiet" box. Items like paper to color or write on, calm music to listen to, treasures she has collected such as seashells or snow globes all can encourage resting, gratitude, and wonderment of life.

Chapter Seven

WHEN TOOLS GET RUSTY

"It is better to wear out than to rust out." — Richard Cumberland

Yeou have probably given your daughter the same advice you heard from your parents, "Don't just sit there. Do something." But this old cliché may not be the best advice. There are times when she needs to do just the opposite — stop and take care of herself before she can do something. How can she get the most out of life if she is upset, tired, bored, malnourished, or lonely? Each of these "rusts" affects her well-being and must be addressed if she is to have a full, balanced life.

Each day your daughter wakes up to twenty-four brand-new hours. She has the power to choose how her day unfolds. She must include the time to evaluate her mental and physical condition if she is to make clear, competent decisions and maximize her power tools. This daily evaluation provides her the opportunity to rejuvenate, repair, and restore her strength.

If your daughter does not address the rust each day, she will have to spend a significant amount of time in the future making repairs on a weakened body. The minor rusts that she could have repaired with daily maintenance she may find have grown into major corrosions. When your daughter finds that her health has deteriorated, she has no choice of when to fix it — she must take action immediately. The time your daughter spends fixing a worn-down body distracts from making good decisions and finding meaning in life. Also, being forced to deal with a health crisis may alter her priorities. When her health is not what it should be, it is difficult for your daughter to focus on her goals.

Your daughter must take the personal responsibility to take care of herself physically and emotionally. She needs strength to handle life's challenges, and she cannot accomplish her goals in a compromised state. Sound health has to come first.

There are many rusts of the body and mind, but teens are particularly vulnerable to several rusts. The rusts of stress, inadequate sleep, inactivity, poor nutrition, and loneliness detract from your daughter's personal sense of wellness and competence. The following pages offer concrete strategies for daily maintenance and repair that can help your daughter overcome these factors.

The Rust of Stress

"Two rules for stress management: Rule one: Don't sweat the small stuff.
Rule two: It's all small stuff." — Robert Elliot

"So, tell me. What do you do for fun?"

"Fun. I can't remember the last time I had fun!"

This discouraged reply is not the response of a tired, young mother of a preschooler, but Madison, a popular, active sixteen-year-old high school junior. Madison is not exaggerating her predicament. The complexities of school, family life, peers, and her own expectations all add to her hectic life. This busyness leaves Madison feeling powerless and out of control. She is physically exhausted after drill team practice, yet she rushes to her part-time job at the mall. She rarely sits down to start her homework before 10 P.M. This lifestyle is taking a physical and emotional toll on her. She has headaches and occasional stomach upsets, and she is losing weight. The paradox of having a full life entraps Madison in a world that leaves no time for fun.

Madison is not alone. Her story is like that of many teens who struggle with balancing an impossibly busy schedule with much needed downtime. High school counselors are seeing increasing numbers of teen girls who are facing overwhelming daily pressures and the inevitable stress that follows. The rust of stress overload is a consequence of this taxing existence.

Too much stress can take its toll on your daughter's health. Some doctors estimate that over 75 percent of all visits to health-care providers are stress related. Paul Rosch, M.D., president of the American Institute of Stress, notes that stress can cause symptoms such as headaches, shortness of breath, chest tightness, sweating, and dizziness. It also can produce tightened muscles in the neck and shoulders, upset stomach, feelings of irritability, depression, colds, flu, premenstrual syndrome, and insomnia. Stress overload weakens the immune system and can lead to serious problems like hypertension, heart disease, and cancer.

An emotional by-product of stress overload is feeling a lack of control. Like Madison, many teens feel that their life is running them, not that they are running their lives. They feel powerless to manage the daily tasks. This leads to a perception of helplessness that can create anger that, in turn, further feeds stress. It is not so much the busyness of life that causes this destructive cycle, but the feelings of stress and lack of control that impact emotional health.

Another emotional problem associated with stress is feeling alienated and out of sync with family and friends. The necessity to have both parents working and the trend to live away from extended family have left many teens feeling disconnected. This emotional isolation causes them to feel they are just going through the motions, compounding their tensions. Michael Lewis, Ph.D., author and developmental scientist, points out the reasons why more people are feeling the stresses of emotional isolation. "The message of the last twenty years has been to make sure that you are okay. But when you focus on the self, you sacrifice emotional ties to others and the sense of community that is essential to coping well with all sources of stress. There is nothing in society that is bringing us together — politics are diverse and people are always on the move." Today's competitive, mobile society coupled with self-focus has created increased stress for your daughter as well as her peers.

Stress overload can be avoided with the right attitude. There is a choice. Your daughter can choose to be consumed by the stress, or she can choose the "I can" attitude. This pragmatic optimism will allow her to feel in control, which can reduce her stress. Below are a few suggestions that can help your daughter minimize stress:

Incorporate fun and humor into life. Due to its optimistic approach, the power tool of Experiencing the Humor can enable her to feel protected and in control. Humor represents cognitive control. Your daughter cannot control the external world, but she can control how she views it and her emotional response.

Deal directly with the source of the stress and keep things in perspective. When your daughter relies on the guidance of her Connected Inner Guide, she sees the whole picture and can determine appropriate actions. In dealing with the problem, your daughter should concentrate on the things she can handle and try not to exaggerate situations.

Stay connected to friends and family. Ties and bonds to family, friends, and your daughter's community offer stability and support that can lessen stress.

Make extra time. One of the chief complaints given when people are asked about stress is they have too much to do and too little time. By focusing on her goals and prioritizing her actions, your daughter can eliminate distractions and unnecessary activities.

Consider a pet as a source for de-stressing. When your daughter pets her dog or cat, it produces a calming effect. In a study at State University of New York, pulse rates were measured while forty-five women performed math problems. When alone with the researcher, they averaged a pulse rate of one hundred. When joined by their dogs, the pulse rate dropped to seventy and they answered more questions correctly.

Integrate stress busters into the day. Your daughter's taking care of herself involves making time each day to unwind before she unravels. A few stress busters she might enjoy include the following:

- Talking to her Creator — Giving stresses and concerns to a Higher Power can soothe, heal, and restore.

- Meditation — Being still, emptying her mind for at least fifteen minutes each day, can make her open to receive peace.
- Music therapy — Since the beginning of time, music has played an integral role in alleviating stress. Music therapy works on the brain's reaction to various stimuli. Music is known to release endorphins (natural feel-good hormones). Soothing pitch and slow tempo help ease the mind.
- Aromatherapy — Smells also have a therapeutic effect on stress. The calming aroma of Grandma's apple pie baking in the oven brings memories of comfort and security. Research shows that fragrance can affect mood and well-being. Scent receptors in the nose trigger the brain to release neurochemicals that might soothe, relax, and energize.
- Exercise — A physical routine has been shown to reduce stress and improve health. Deep breathing and an increased heart rate improve oxygen flow to the brain and muscles throughout the body. Exercise releases endorphins that produce a feel-good effect, sometimes referred to as a runner's high, that can reduce stress.
- Yoga — Yoga energizes the body through breathing to promote relaxation and concentration. It uses meditation to reduce stress and promote a positive attitude. Yoga offers a physical workout to energize and stabilize, and it incorporates visualization to create a relaxed, uplifted state.
- Progressive muscle relaxation — Muscle relaxation recognizes and counters muscular tension. Tapes are usually used to direct gradual tensing and relaxing of specific muscle groups in a progression from hands to feet and throughout body.
- Guided imagery — Guided mental imagery focuses the mind and offers a calm, safe retreat away from present stress. A leader or a tape directs soothing mental imagery, often depicting a special place that provides a mental escape.
- Soothing surroundings — Controlled, calm, private surroundings afford more relaxation than those that are not. Work and sleep areas

should have minimal noise and soothing sounds, soft textured surfaces, and warm lighting, not fluorescent. Plants or window views overlooking a natural setting can also have calming effects.

■ Good habits — Soothe stress by developing lifetime habits of getting enough sleep, exercising anxiety away, and emphasizing good nutrition.

Studies have shown that each of these techniques can reduce stress and improve health. When your daughter alleviates the rust of stress overload, she will feel more in control of her life.

Keep in mind that not all stress is bad. Whether your daughter is trying out for a team or is studying for an exam, a certain amount of stress allows her to handle situations better. Small quantities of stress trigger alertness and an "on" mode that is her body's way of meeting new challenges. As stress increases, so does effectiveness up to a point. When your daughter passes this point, too much stress causes her performance level to decrease, and your daughter suffers from the stress that initially enabled her. At this point stress becomes a rust that corrodes your daughter's quality of life.

Stress is a normal part of everyday life. No life is stress free. It is important to recognize when good stress becomes bad. While individual tolerance levels to stress vary, when your daughter discovers how much stress is helpful to her, she can use it to her advantage and not let it become rust in her toolbox.

Tips from the Toolbox

When you detect that your daughter is feeling overloaded from being too busy, you may want to discuss with her some of the following questions:

- *What do you like about each of your activities?*
- *What do you not like about being involved in them?*
- *Does the activity fit in with your mission and vision?*
- *Does the activity help to reduce your stress?*
- *Do the benefits outweigh the disadvantages?*

Many times, this will be enough for her to see what needs to stay and what can go. You can help your daughter reduce stress by evaluating her goals and priorities in choosing her activities.

The Rust of Inadequate Sleep

"Sleep is that golden chain that ties health and our bodies together."
— Thomas Dekker

Teens need more sleep than they are getting. A study conducted in Illinois among Evanston high school students showed that students recorded eight to ten hours of sleep in the summer, but only seven hours of sleep during the school year. This study supports statistical information that shows that most teenagers are only getting about seven hours of sleep, but require about nine hours to be completely rested. Teens' busy schedules and their unique sleep patterns both exacerbate this sleep deficit.

Teens today have an increase in demands on their time. A part-time job, late-night studying, and even routines that schools and parents encourage contribute to teens' loss of needed sleep. A 1998 survey by Mary A. Carskadon, Ph.D., director of chronobiology at E. P. Bradley Hospital at Brown University's School of Medicine, found that 59 percent of teens surveyed had part-time jobs, 20 percent spent at least twenty hours a week doing extracurricular activities, and many, 65 percent of the girls and 38 percent of the boys, get up before 6 A.M. on school mornings.

The onset of puberty adds to the complexity of this problem. According to Dr. Richard Allen, founder of the Johns Hopkins Sleep Disorders Clinic, who studies the relationship of sleep to teens' academic performance, puberty alters teens' sleep patterns. Due to their biological clocks, teens are less alert earlier in the day, becoming more alert just as their school day ends. This may be attributed to a biological fact. James B. Maas, Ph.D., author of *Power Sleep*, notes that melatonin, the natural sleep-inducing hormone of the brain, does not get secreted in a teen's brain until 1 or 2 A.M. This may explain why teens are not sleepy earlier in the night, and why they seem to need more sleep in the morning.

Interestingly enough, schools generally start earlier for teens than younger children. Dr. Allen observes, "The kids who get less sleep during the school week have worse grades. It is difficult to learn a new concept when you are sleepy. You can't learn algebra while falling asleep." Scientists have discovered a link between sleep and memory. It has been shown that memory is improved with the last stage of sleep known as the REM (rapid eye movement) phase. This last ninety minutes of the sleep cycle, long recognized as the most restful stage, has also been shown to improve memory recall. Something as simple as getting a full night's sleep can help your daughter's memory as well as her grades and feelings of rest and well-being.

Educators and legislators are beginning to take seriously the unique sleep requirements for teens. One suburban Minneapolis school effectively dealt with this problem by changing their starting time from 7:20 A.M. to 8:30 A.M. and found that this resulted in significantly higher standardized test scores and fewer behavior problems. They linked academic improvement at this school directly to their students getting more rest. There has also been legislation in the U.S. House of Representatives that would offer school districts financial incentives to change school hours to synchronize with teenagers' body clocks. Studies have clearly shown that early school start times are frequently associated with sleep deprivation, which can cause poor academic performance and increase the risk for accidents and injuries, especially for teen drivers.

Many parents warn their daughters about the danger of drinking and driving, but fail to warn them of the hazard of driving while tired. More teens die because of sleep loss than alcohol in auto accidents. Driving while fatigued is a common problem. According to the U.S. National Highway Traffic Safety Administration, sleep deprivation is the primary cause of at least 100,000 crashes and more than 1,500 deaths annually. Young people are the largest at-risk group for drowsy driving and fall-asleep crashes. A National Sleep Foundation survey found that

72 percent of eighteen- to twenty-four-year-olds admitted having driven while tired. And 33 percent of adults between the ages of eighteen and twenty-nine reported falling asleep at the wheel within the last year.

Each day, many Americans are functionally handicapped by sleep deprivation. Over one-third of Americans complain of daytime fatigue. Lack of sleep and the impaired judgment that accompanies it have become an accepted part of every day life. This unhealthy cycle rusts your daughter's physical and emotional well-being. Although fatigue is a pervasive problem, it can be simply remedied. Here are a few suggestions to combat this rust:

Encourage your daughter to get enough sleep. If she goes to bed at the same time every night, she can establish a routine that will help her fall asleep easier. Bedtime rituals and habits offer a predictable pattern that can condition her body for sleep.

Create an environment conducive to sleep with a good mattress, a dark cool room, and a secure atmosphere. Your daughter's bedding and room surroundings should be a priority investment.

Your daughter can learn strategies to minimize nightly distractions. Addressing worries earlier in the day helps to reduce the time it takes to fall asleep. If she wakes up during the night with a concern, she might jot it down and deal with it the next day.

Setting priorities and establishing goals will help keep your daughter from overcommitting herself. It is valuable for her to learn to say no to demands on her time. There will always be good opportunities vying for her time, but she must learn to distinguish the good from the best. She may refer to her power tool of Designing Your Lifetime Strategic Plan to help make these decisions. When she is not overcommitted, she can set aside enough time to adequately rest.

Help your daughter realize that her lost sleep cannot be regained. Many teens unsuccessfully try to make up for lost sleep by sleeping later on weekends. But staying up late and sleeping in on weekends creates a pattern that can cause difficulty in falling asleep on school nights.

Sleep deprivation jeopardizes your daughter's decision-making ability and reduces the control she has over her life. It is hard for your daughter's Connected Inner Guide to rely on its memory and judgment when lack of sleep clouds reasoning power and increases emotional volatility. When she is fatigued, decisions become more difficult, and her competency is compromised. Because competency wanes, so does her sense of control. When sleep deprivation jeopardizes decision making, it becomes a rust for the Connected Inner Guide.

How can you be sure that your daughter is getting enough sleep? Here is a quiz for your daughter, from Dr. Maas's *Power Sleep,* that may help her determine if she is getting enough. An answer of "T" ("true") to two or more of the following statements may be a sign of sleep problems:

T or F   I need an alarm clock to wake up at the appropriate time.

T or F   It's a struggle for me to get out of bed in the morning.

T or F   Weekday mornings I hit the snooze button several times to get more sleep.

T or F   I feel tired, irritable, and stressed out during the week.

T or F   I have trouble concentrating and remembering.

T or F   I feel slow with critical thinking, problem solving, and being creative.

T or F   I often fall asleep watching television.

T or F   I often fall asleep after heavy meals.

T or F   I often fall asleep within five minutes of getting into bed.

T or F   I often feel drowsy while driving.

T or F   I often sleep extra hours on weekend mornings.

T or F   I often need a nap to get through the day.

T or F   I have dark circles around my eyes.

 Tips from the Toolbox

Your daughter's schedule must include downtime. Being able to relax can help her go to sleep more quickly. Dr. Herbert Benson, author of The Relaxation Response, *describes a quick relaxation*

exercise that can prompt sleep. Sit comfortably with your eyes closed, and begin a progressive tightening and releasing of major muscle groups. Start at your toes and work your way up to your head. You may want think of a favorite place or repeat a favorite word or phrase, while you let negative thoughts drift away. The point is to let your imagination take you away from worry and back to your relaxed state. Taking just five or ten minutes each day to relax can be an effective way to induce sleep.

The Rust of Inactivity

"Laziness grows on people; it begins in cobwebs and ends in iron chains. The more one has to do, the more he is able to accomplish." — Thomas Buxton

The Tin Woodsman in *The Wizard of Oz* spent years trapped in the rust of inactivity. The longer he was frozen in place, the more impossible he found it to move. The Woodsman could not pursue his dream of having a heart as long as he was paralyzed with rust. His inactivity incapacitated his ability to help himself. As Dorothy oiled the frozen, rusted joints of his body and he began to move, he became flexible and free. The Tin Woodsman's desire to continue to be active and his movements enabled him to overcome the rusts that once threatened his existence.

Like the Tin Woodsman, an inactive lifestyle deprives your daughter of many life-enriching experiences. Inactivity can rob her of long- and short-term benefits that include good health, social interaction, and feelings of energy, balance, and overall well-being.

Exercise is an activity that can remedy this rust. If your daughter develops the habit of exercising when she is young, it can make a big difference later in her life. Girls who exercise are less likely to develop heart disease, pulmonary disease, or back and bone problems when they get older.

Health problems such as allergies, asthma, obesity, menstrual disorders, sleep difficulties, and arthritis have also been associated with insufficient exercise. Although inactivity has been linked to grave physical and psychological problems, many of these problems can be alleviated to some degree with exercise.

Girls need exercise, and one way to accomplish this is through participation in organized sports. According to Girl Tech, a company dedicated to encouraging girls in technology use, girls who participate in sports are three times more likely to graduate from high school, 80 percent less likely to have an unwanted pregnancy, 92 percent less likely to use drugs, and 40 to 60 percent less likely to get breast cancer. Girls who participate in sports often become successful adults. Eighty percent of women who are key leaders in Fortune 500 companies have a background in sports. Girls who are involved in sports make good leaders, have a healthy outlook on life, and know their own value. And girls who exercise usually become women who exercise.

Research consistently reports that athletes have greater self-worth than nonathletes. Playing sports can help provide a feeling of belonging. In terms of psychological benefits, loneliness and isolation diminish in a team setting. The positive group associations of a team that shares values and common goals can offer protection from loneliness and validation of self-worth.

Although sport participation offers many benefits, your daughter may want to find another form of exercise if she is not athletically inclined. To remove the rust of inactivity, she should find an exercise that she likes and will continue. She doesn't have to run a 10-K race or swim two hours a day. Research has shown that any kind of exercise she finds enjoyable will offer benefits.

Exercise affects not only health and emotional well-being but also attitude. Getting fit takes discipline and a take-charge, "I can" attitude. Each time that your daughter exercises, she proves she has accomplished something positive and builds confidence. Getting fit helps your daughter prove to herself that she is personally responsible for her health and that she can reach her goals.

The confidence that comes from reaching fitness goals expands to other parts of her life. Exercise and teamwork help girls to have better self-esteem, less depression, and a better image of their bodies. Generally, physically fit people are more intelligent, emotionally stable, self-confident, and relaxed.

Even a simple activity like walking has been shown to increase self-esteem, positive feelings, and psychological well-being, while decreasing anxiety, negativity, and anger.

Tips from the Toolbox

One walking technique your daughter might find effective is a combination of walking and relaxation. At the University of Massachusetts School of Medicine, a team experimented with walking and relaxation by counting steps or repeating a word or phrase as each foot hit the ground. The object was to keep their minds from dwelling on anything that caused tension. This combination of walking and relaxation produced two important results: It brought a reduction in anxiety for the participants and it improved their mood. With this technique, the euphoric feeling that normally occurred between the third to fifth mile of walking or running was generated with the first mile of relaxation/walking.

WHO EXERCISES?

According to the President's Council on Fitness and Sports, a person is more likely to get regular exercise if she

- Enjoys physical activity and believes that time can be found or made for exercise

- Believes the benefits of exercise outweigh the costs

- Has friends or family members who exercise or who support her getting exercise

- Feels safe exercising outdoors and has access to an attractive and convenient outdoor exercise space

- Has access to convenient and affordable exercise facilities or programs or has quality exercise equipment at home.

The Rust of Poor Nutrition

"HALT — Don't get too hungry, angry, lonely, or tired."
— Overeaters Anonymous acronym

"There she is — Miss America." And who is she? There is a strong chance that she is a person that the World Health Organization would categorize as malnourished. According to research published in the *Journal of the American Medical Association,* a significant number of contestant winners over the past twenty years had below normal body mass indexes, and an increasing number had body mass indexes of less than 18.5, the World Health Organization's standard for undernutrition. To some, the whole idea of a beauty pageant is a joke, but over 10 million people watched the Miss America contest in 1999. For many young women, this model of thinness is their standard for beauty.

Thin is in and our daughters are in danger. This distorted image of the perfect body adds to feelings of insecurity and faltering self-worth in young women. Many teens feel out of control due to this insecurity and may compensate by a misguided drive to control their eating habits. This desire for control makes young women particularly vulnerable to the devastating diseases of eating disorders such as anorexia, bulimia, and compulsive overeating. Failing to eat healthfully makes young women's bodies susceptible to many rusts. Overeating, crash dieting, and poor nutrition in general are serious problems for many girls.

Poor nutrition is a physical and emotional stressor. Fatigue, irritability, impaired judgment, and stress are a few complications produced by not eating well. It is important to realize the connection between food and general well-being. When your daughter's body meets baseline nutritional needs, she is better equipped to handle life.

As teens get older, they assume more control over the foods that they eat. Jobs and other after-school activities, as well as changes in traditional family lifestyles, have caused teens to increasingly make decisions for their diet. At a time when their nutritional needs are the greatest, ironically, they may be getting less than what they need.

Your daughter requires extra nutrients during the adolescent growth spurt, which begins around age ten, peaks near age twelve, and is completed at about age fifteen, according to the International Food Information Council. This intensive growth period brings dramatic increases in height as well as hormonal changes affecting every body organ, including the brain. Vitamin A, beta-carotene, iron, and calcium are particularly necessary during this growth period for your daughter. Iron is especially important with the onset of menstruation in girls. The recommended daily allowance for iron is 12 to 15 milligrams (mg) a day. Increases in skeletal mass boost a young woman's requirements for calcium to about 1,200 mg a day. Since approximately half of her bone structure is deposited during adolescence, calcium is vital. Even when she has completed her growth, calcium is still necessary because the mineral continues to be deposited in her bones.

Food is not only necessary to fuel the body, but can affect your daughter's mood. What your daughter eats can make her feel better or worse. Some foods promote calmness, others pep up the body. Complex carbohydrates such as pasta, popcorn, pretzels, and bread trigger the brain to release serotonin-carrying hormones that promote rest, while protein and fat are signals for the body to brace itself for work and tension. Proteins such as tuna, chicken, burgers, peanut butter, and low-fat yogurt rev up the body by reducing serotonin in the brain and by providing energy.

When your daughter is under stress, what she eats can aggravate the condition. Teens have a tendency when they are tense to snack on comfort foods that are high in fat and sugar. But these foods may cause them to feel worse. Fats and sugars are slow to digest, sap energy, pile on the pounds, and probably lack key nutrients like vitamins A, C, and calcium, according to Susan Male Smith, R.D., author of the article "Food: The New Stress Therapy." By avoiding stress-intensifying foods, your daughter can cope with situations better.

An added benefit to eating nutritionally is better decision-making ability for your daughter. When she eats healthy, well-balanced foods, her cognition and attention improve. Her Connected Inner Guide is better able to think clearly and evaluate her choices, which lead to better decisions and increased self-confidence. The secret to a healthy diet is variety and balance. Eating well prevents your daughter from having to spend time repairing the effects of poor nutrition. She is then free to address more satisfying pursuits.

SEVEN TIPS TO BETTER NUTRITION

Here are some simple rules that insure sound nutrition:

- Avoid crash diets, diet pills, or quick weight-loss schemes.
- Be patient when trying to lose weight.
- Drink plenty of water or other fluids.
- Take vitamin supplements.
- Never skip meals in an effort to lose weight.
- Increase physical activity.
- Eat a variety of foods.

 Tips from the Toolbox

Here are twelve foods recommended by Sandy and Harry Choron, authors of The Book of Lists for Kids, *that your daughter may want to eat before taking a test. They won't make her smarter, but can keep her alert by fighting the affects of carbohydrates (candy, bread, sugar) that tend to make her sleepy. Try broccoli, apples, grapes, nuts, pears, lean beef, peaches, skim milk, fish, low-fat yogurt, peanuts, and turkey breast for mental energy.*

The Rust of Loneliness

"You cannot be lonely if you like the person you're alone with." — Wayne Dyer

Preps, geeks, freaks, Goths, or jocks — the names may change, but the concept stays the same. Look alike or look different, rebel or conform — the motive is the same. Belong and fit in. The obvious solution to avoid being alone for many teens is to belong to a group. The avoidance of loneliness is a primary underlying motivation for selecting a group of friends. Teens join groups to feel accepted, to reduce anxiety, and to get an identity they feel comfortable with. The groups they join can vary from drama clubs to volunteer associations to juvenile gangs. Whatever their nature, teen groups are avenues for teens to avoid loneliness.

Belonging to a group, however, does not guarantee a teen will avoid feeling lonely, and conversely, not belonging to a group does not guarantee they will be lonely. Being lonely has little to do with being alone. A teenager can be in a relationship and feel alone. She can be in a crowd and feel alone. Loneliness is a distressing awareness of not feeling connected with others and that certain needs are not being met.

Loneliness is one of the most painful and potent forces in a teenager's life. Feelings of loneliness are a primary motivator for many of their actions. In fact, many teens will avoid loneliness at all cost. They may make poor choices and live with undesirable consequences in an attempt to avoid being lonely. Dr. Michael Riera, in his book *Uncommon Sense for Parents with Teenagers,* states, "To understand why certain risky behaviors are worthwhile for adolescents takes a little digging on the part of parents. The main consequence of saying 'no' to negative peer pressure is not just withstanding the 'heat of the moment' as most adults think. Rather, it is coping with a sense of exclusion as others engage in the behavior and leave the adolescent increasingly alone. It is the loss of shared experience. Further, the sense of exclusion remains whenever the group later recounts what happened. This feeling of loneliness then becomes pervasive, and carries an easy solution — go along with the crowd."

In the extreme case, "the crowd" may be a gang. Research has shown that teens who were more likely to join gangs had lower levels of self-esteem and felt less in control of their lives than their nongang peers. Despite their negative image, gangs give insecure teens an opportunity for feeling in control and accepted. Even gangs that are involved in antisocial behavior often fill the gap of loneliness.

You may or may not be aware if your daughter is feeling lonely, but note some risk factors that make her more prone to feeling lonely. Experiencing a death in the immediate family, a parental divorce, a sibling leaving home, illness of a family member, a fight with a girlfriend or boyfriend, rejection by peers, and moving to a new town all leave her more susceptible to the rust of loneliness. There is a tendency to engage in certain behaviors when a teen suffers from loneliness that may exacerbate the problem. The following behaviors may be a red flag that your daughter is not handling her loneliness well:

- She is overly critical of her physical appearance.
- She assumes no one likes her.
- She makes no attempt to get involved in social activities.
- She becomes self-conscious and worries about being evaluated by others.
- She appears to have difficulty expressing feelings and engaging in assertive behavior.
- She seems afraid to stand up and say no to unreasonable requests.
- She generally avoids taking social risks and meeting people.
- She has difficulty expressing personal beliefs, making phone calls, and participating in group activities.
- She expects others to reject her.
- She seems to feel isolated, alone, and unhappy.

These behaviors are not a constructive way for your daughter to effectively handle her loneliness. Your daughter should know that loneliness does not have to be a permanent state. If your daughter is feeling lonely, she needs to feel warmth, understanding, and support from her family and friends.

Loneliness can be overcome but it depends on your daughter. Her greatest assets in combating loneliness are her power tools. The power tool of Adjusting Your Mirror helps her generate a positive attitude about herself. When your daughter likes herself, she is comfortable being alone. Designing her Lifetime Strategic Plan gives your daughter a sense of direction and purpose in her life that puts loneliness into perspective. When she focuses on her goals and dreams, feelings of loneliness do not seem as important. Expanding Your Limits enables her to try new experiences and take social risks to meet people. Experiencing the Humor alters her perspective to view lonely situations less seriously. The power tool of Gratitude helps her unearth her hidden treasures and realize the good in her life. Appreciating the small things allows her to overcome the negative effect of loneliness. Cultivating Unconditional Love helps her to realize her innate worthiness. Loving herself unconditionally and knowing she is loved unconditionally bolsters her con-fidence. And ultimately, the power tool of Resting in Spirituality reminds your daughter that she is never alone. As your daughter uses these power tools, if she remembers to fuel the tools with the "I can" attitude of pragmatic optimism, she will have the strength and confidence to overcome loneliness. Your daughter should focus on three areas of her life to combat loneliness:

- Develop friendships. Your daughter can fill the empty spot of loneliness with the best people she can find.
- Nurture existing relationships. She should build on positive

---

THREE STEPS TO OVERCOMING PEER PRESSURE

According to counselor and author Sharon Scott in her book *Peer Pressure Reversal,* there is a simple method to avoid going along with the crowd when it can be harmful.

1. Check out the scene. Notice and identify trouble.

2. Make a good decision. Understand and choose consequences.

3. Act to avoid trouble. Take effective action.

relationships she already has, such as relatives, teachers, teammates, and others.

■ Work on herself. By focusing on internal growth, she can learn to like herself and become comfortable with herself when she is lonely.

As your daughter matures, she still needs the unconditional love of family, but her peers are now the primary influence on her sense of belonging. Peers, more than family, provide the sense of acceptance, prestige, belonging, and approval that combat loneliness. But searching for acceptance from any external source will not prove satisfying. The void of loneliness can be temporarily filled by others, but in the long run, your daughter can only satisfy this need by learning to be content with herself. A positive sense of identity gives her the confidence to wisely choose a group that shares her values and accepts her for herself. Since a positive self-image makes your daughter more comfortable with herself, it can be an immunization against the devastation of loneliness.

Ten Strategies to Remove the Rust

When too much stress, inadequate sleep, inactivity, poor nutrition, or loneliness weakens your daughter's health, she needs to address the problem promptly. Left unattended, rust grows, and ultimately, becomes a corrosion that compromises your daughter's decision-making ability and her quality of life.

Your daughter must take care of herself both inside and out to keep her toolbox in shape. This can be complicated because she may not recognize when rust is beginning to form. If your daughter doesn't recognize the problem, she won't be able to repair it. And if she allows the rust to accumulate, it will be more difficult for her to fix. Although your daughter must do most of this work on her own, you can help her address the problem. Here are ten strategies you can employ to help your daughter identify, avoid, reduce, or remove the rusts that she will inevitably encounter:

1. **Listen.** Listening is the most important part of a conversation with your daughter. You can learn about her and even from her. Nothing builds her self-worth like knowing you care about what she has to say.

2. **Ask the right questions.** "What do you think you should do?" is generally more effective than stating what you think, and it allows your daughter to practice using her Connected Inner Guide.

3. **Be available.** Even if it isn't obvious, your daughter appreciates your presence. Knowing that you are available if needed offers her security.

4. **Empathize.** Her problems are very real to her and should not be minimized. It may be helpful if you have had a similar situation to share your experience with her.

5. **Let her know that you value her.** Tell your daughter often that you value specific characteristics, and point out what they are. Be careful not to compare her with others. She will feel more valued if you compliment her unique qualities.

6. **Be a good role model.** Deal with the rusts in your own life, and focus on acting with integrity in the moment of choice.

7. **Don't sweat the small stuff.** Evaluate situations using the big picture perspective and teach your daughter to do the same.

8. **Spend time with your daughter individually.** Privacy increases her comfort level and helps her to feel valued.

9. **Provide information and resources** about the rusts of stress, inadequate sleep, inactivity, poor nutrition, and loneliness. You may not know when your daughter will need the information, but if it is available, she can educate herself on the possible pitfalls and prevent or correct them.

10. **If you become very concerned, seek appropriate help.** Most communities have a wealth of mental and physical health resources available for you and your daughter.

One of the best ways you can help your daughter handle the typical rusts of life is to help her recognize the rust before it becomes corrosion. By emphasizing the importance of and teaching her strategies to lessen stress, get enough sleep, become physical fit, eat properly, and feel a sense of belonging, you give her the tools and information she needs to successfully combat the rusts.

Even if the rust develops into a full-blown corrosion, it is not too late to reverse its adverse effects. Unquestionably, certain rusts will require more diligence than others will, but they all can be fixed. With the right attitude, motivation, and tools, your daughter can restore and maintain her physical and mental well-being.

The secret is balance and moderation. As with most of life, extremes often create problems. Too much sleep is just as problematic as not getting enough. Time alone must be balanced with social interaction. And in the case of stress, some is necessary for motivation and energy to accomplish tasks. If one element of your daughter's health and well-being is neglected or overstated, the other components suffer as well. Balance is the key to keeping her tools free from rust.

With the Connected Inner Guide and the power tools, your daughter has the basics for a well-rounded life. By keeping her toolbox well maintained, she guarantees that her tools will be ready and in working order when she needs them.

HONING THE SKILLS
What You Can Do

Conducting a Stress Check — *These questions can determine ways you can help your daughter reduce her stress.*

Is your family so busy that you have little down time? Do you take time out of each day to listen to your daughter? Are you reasonable in what you expect from your daughter? Do you try to lessen your daughter's stress when you can? What steps can you take to alleviate stress in your family?

Taking the Quiz "What Is Your Sleep IQ?" — *This quiz published by the National Sleep Foundation (© 1998 NSF) can help you assess your knowledge about sleep.*

Are the following statements true or false?

1. During sleep, your brain rests.
2. You cannot learn to function normally with one or two fewer hours of sleep a night than you need.
3. Boredom makes you feel sleepy, even if you have had enough sleep.
4. Resting in bed with your eyes closed cannot satisfy your body's need for sleep.
5. Snoring is not harmful as long as it doesn't disturb others or wake you up.
6. Everyone dreams every night.
7. The older you get, the fewer hours of sleep you need.
8. Most people don't know when they are sleepy.
9. Raising the volume of your radio will help you stay awake while driving.
10. Sleep disorders are mainly due to worry or psychological problems.

11. The human body never adjusts to night-shift work.

12. Most sleep disorders go away even without treatment.

Scoring

Answers: (1-F, 2-T, 3-F, 4-T, 5-F, 6-T, 7-F, 8-T, 9-F, 10-F, 11-T, 12-F)

11–12 correct: Congratulations, you're a sleep genius!

8–10 correct: Not bad! Learn more facts about sleep to improve your life.

4–7 correct: Study the answers above and you'll see why sleep is so important.

1–3 correct: It's never too late to learn about sleep. Why not start now?

Copyright © 1998, National Sleep Foundation

What You Can Do with Your Older Daughter (Ages Thirteen to Twenty-Three)

Using Strategies for Proper Nutrition in Today's Fast-Food Society — *This discussion will make your daughter aware of better food options when she is eating out.*

Discuss with your daughter her three favorite fast-food restaurants. Go through their menus and talk with her about the healthy foods that are listed. Knowing she has options at her favorite places may help her make healthier choices.

Getting a Good Night's Sleep — *This assignment will show your daughter how much sleep she is getting and where her sleep habits need improvement.*

Have your daughter keep a sleep diary for one week. Record the time she goes to bed and the time she wakes, and any circumstances that prevent her from getting a good night's sleep. Note the days that she is getting the recommended nine hours of sleep per night. Can she make adjustments in her schedule that will allow her to get more rest?

Learning from Your Experiences — *This exercise will help your daughter recognize the difference between being nice and being a pushover.*

1. Your coach asks you to pick up the equipment after practice for the fifth day straight. You
   A. Do it even though you will be late to your next class.
   B. Respectfully point out that several of your teammates have never picked up after practice, and ask to be excused.

2. Your friend is always late, no matter what you do. You are tired of missing the first few minutes of a movie. You
   A. Wait outside the movie, no matter how long it takes.
   B. Wait until the movie starts and go inside.

3. A friend calls to chat on the phone and you are waiting for another call. You
   A. Continue to talk, hoping the other person will call back.
   B. Tell your friend you will call her back at a better time.

4. A mother that you seldom baby-sit for has unruly children that you cannot control. She asks you to baby-sit. You
   A. Say yes. After all, it's not that often.
   B. Say no, but suggest an older sitter.

5. When someone asks you for a favor, and you must decline, you
   A. Say yes anyway, and figure you will work it out.
   B. Tell her you would like to help, but won't be able to this time.

6. You and your friend are in charge of cleanup after a meeting. You need to go home, but your friend lingers at the door visiting with the others. You
   A. Clean up by yourself, not wanting to cause a scene.
   B. Explain that you need her help so you can go home.

7. You are hosting a "girls only" party at your house. Your friend calls and asks to bring her boyfriend. You
   A. Tell her to go ahead, knowing this will change many of your plans for the evening.
   B. Tell her you are sorry, but it is a "girls only" party.

8. Your friend asks to borrow your new skirt. She has not returned other clothes she has borrowed. You

   A. Let her borrow the skirt so you can stay on good terms.

   B. Tell her that you would be happy to let her borrow it as soon as she returns the other clothes.

9. You have an argument with your boyfriend and you know he is wrong. You

   A. Cave in just to end the fight.

   B. Stick to your guns and explain why you are upset.

10. You realize that your science teacher has graded your paper wrong, giving you a letter grade point difference. You

   A. Don't say anything. You could make her mad.

   B. Point out the mistake, tactfully asking her to correct it.

Scoring

2 points for every "A" answer.

1 point for every "B" answer.

If you score 18–20 points, you may be a pushover. You often accommodate others at your own expense, perhaps in an effort to be liked. Remember, relying on your Connected Inner Guide in making decisions is more important than pleasing everyone.

If you score 14–17 points, you are nice, but you may occasionally let your Crybaby Heart talk you into actions out of misplaced guilt. Remember, being nice does not mean being a pushover.

If you score 12–13 points, you probably have balanced your Connected Inner Guide's needs with the needs of others. You are adept at evaluating decisions in the moment of choice and not afraid to be nice.

What You Can Do with Your Younger Daughter (Ages Six to Twelve)

Conducting a Nutritional Search — *This game will start your daughter thinking about which foods are good for her and which are not.*

Watch a television show with your daughter and count the number of commercials that promote healthy foods. Count the commercials that promote junk foods. Together, take a magazine and cut out pictures of nutritious foods. Now, plan a nutritious meal together and have her help prepare it.

Exercising Every Day — *This activity will help your daughter develop a habit of exercise early in her life.*

Follow a routine of physical exercise with your daughter. For instance, ride a bike, walk, play ball, skip rope, or dance. Whether you choose one activity or a combination, be sure to exercise every day.

Becoming a Social Animal — *These exercises will help your daughter combat loneliness, and she may even make a new friend.*

- Say hi to five new people today. Remember to smile.
- Notice someone who needs your help in your class or neighborhood. Offer to help.
- If you see someone being teased, left out, or called a name, how could you help her?
- Don't forget that family members can alleviate loneliness, too. Have your daughter make a regular date with a relative and let her help plan the activity.

Chapter Eight

EQUIPPED FOR LIFE
Building Strength, Confidence, and Integrity

"People grow through experience if they meet life honestly and courageously. This is how character is built." — Eleanor Roosevelt

As your daughter progresses through the strategies in this book, you probably will notice an increase in her confidence and competence. Feel good about your role in helping her become the strong, confident, honorable woman you always envisioned. By equipping her with the tools found in this book, you have given her the ultimate gift. You have given her the means to gain wisdom, courage, and honor.

Your daughter will be able to take her tools with her wherever life takes her. From this moment on, she will have at her disposal tools that will guide her on her journey. These tools travel well and only get stronger with use. Whether she is a preteen deciding which group to associate with or an older teen applying for her first job, her tools will assist her. Whether she is a twenty-four-year-old returning to college or a young mother of two making child-care decisions, her toolbox will still provide the means to obtain strength, confidence and integrity. Whether she is a Fortune 500 CEO making financial and ethical decisions that affect thousands or a middle-aged woman who is simultaneously taking care of her children and her parents, her toolbox will be her rock. And even after you are gone, when she is a retired widow living on a fixed income, her toolbox will equip her to handle any situation she faces.

With each decision, your daughter shapes her life. What she chooses in her moment of choice determines her success. How she uses, how she cares for, and whether she chooses to carry her toolbox is up to her. She can have what she wants, or she can focus on the excuses and reasons why she can't — the choice is hers.

Now that your daughter is equipped with her toolbox, she must proceed with the work at hand — building a life filled with strength, confidence, and integrity. She builds a life of strength mostly by relying on her Connected Inner Guide and her power tools, and also by developing a support team. She builds a life of confidence based on making incrementally better decisions and using her strengths. She builds a life of integrity by relying on her principles and values to construct a wall of honor. By structuring her life on these foundations, she will experience the joys and rewards of being a toolbox-equipped woman.

Building Strength

- -

"There are admirable potentialities in every human being. Believe in your strength and your youth. Learn to repeat endlessly to yourself, 'It all depends on me.'"
— André Gide

Your daughter's best source of strength comes from within. This book emphasizes exactly how your daughter can build this inner fortress. Her Connected Inner Guide, coupled with her power tools, gives her the awareness, wisdom, and determination to behave with integrity. However, some external sources fortify her internal strength.

Everywhere your daughter looks, there are lessons she can learn and people she can learn from. Books, seminars, radio programs, television shows, computer-generated information, educational courses, and networking with a variety of people are sources that augment her inner strength. Of these, networking with people is perhaps her most valuable resource.

Many people interact with your daughter, offer feedback, and provide a wide range of additional information for her. If she will view this as an opportunity to learn, she can assess others' strengths and target specific skills or characteristics that can benefit her. As she identifies areas where she needs help, she can flag certain people who have strengths in these areas to be a part of her resource team. This also can open her eyes to those like her who are struggling with the same difficulties and help her develop strategies to work through situations. These people can point out the pitfalls that they have successfully navigated, or direct her to people that can. Her select resource team can bolster her strength through its support and wisdom by mentoring, instructing, admonishing, helping, counseling, and backing her.

Your daughter should carefully choose her team to optimize its effectiveness. She can choose to include a parent, relative, friend, teacher, counselor, coach, pastor, and certainly, other toolbox-equipped women. Your daughter will want to seek out positive people for her resource team. Dr. Max More, in "Dynamic Optimism," advises people to seek out those who "inspire, support, and assist, not those that discourage, distract, and undermine.... Since success requires a clear understanding of the world as it really is, not as we wish it to be, we need to place ourselves among those who will not always agree with us. If we hear only agreement from those who think just like us, we will fall into a distorted view of the world. Our beliefs, values, and goals need to be tested, questioned, challenged."

In addition to selecting an optimal resource team, your daughter needs to pick her friends carefully. If your daughter hangs out every Friday night with negative people who sulk about how their lives supposedly stink, she will find it difficult to be optimistic and will need to maintain more vigilance over her thinking. She should consider what kind of influence these people have on her. What would happen if she associated with successful, positive people? As the saying goes, "Birds of a feather flock together." Even though she may not consider these people on her resource team, they do have an influence on her. The kind of person your daughter associates with is the kind of person she is likely to become.

Your daughter can learn many characteristics and skills by having diverse team members. In selecting and maintaining her resource team, she will want to consider several factors:

- She should identify people who can make a dramatic difference in her future.

- She should view each member of her resource team as a learning partner who can coach her on specific skills.

- She should not be afraid to step out of her box and seek people who are different than her.

- She probably should not tell her team members that they are on her official resource team because this might intimidate them.

- She should be considerate of their time. Simply by asking their advice about a specific issue, your daughter can gain the necessary insight.

- She should realize that her resource team might change over time, increasing or decreasing in importance and scope, as people come into her life and sometimes fade into the background.

After your daughter has picked her team, she should look for opportunities to spend time with them and study their strengths. By examining their experiences, she can gain valuable insight into what may work for her.

Once your daughter has assembled her support team, how can she best use it? She will want to ask for their help, then listen to their advice, correction, and praise. Then, she should assess the validity of their points. Are they accurate? In what ways? How can she use this information constructively? The choice and the decision-making power are still hers.

It is interesting to note that many influential women rely on a support team as a source of wisdom. Diane Sawyer, news anchor and television journalist, chose inspirational writer Catherine Marshall, as her mentor. As a teen, Sawyer was inspired by a speech given by Marshall in which she expressed, "You have set goals for yourselves. I have heard some of them. But I don't think you have set them high enough. You have talent and intelligence and a chance. I think you should take those goals and expand them. Think of the most you could do with your lives. Make what you do matter. Above all, dream big." Sawyer valued this advice and chose to develop a relationship with Catherine Marshall. She realized the importance of having this inspirational woman on her resource team, and she continued to learn from her until Marshall's death in 1983.

Another influential woman, the United Nations High Commissioner for Refugees Sadako Ogata, notes the value of a resource team. In a 1999 interview at the Institute of International Studies at UC Berkeley, she observed, "You have to make decisions....I think before deciding it is important that you listen to a lot of colleagues who come up with recommendations and advice, but at the end you do have to decide." Sadako Ogata realized that while the decision was still hers, consulting others gave her a broader reference on which to base the decision.

Throughout time, many have realized the value of relying on others' opinions. If your daughter lacks certain experiences and wants to learn faster than she could on her own, she can benefit from consulting others. If she believes she can learn in some way from the experiences of others, she can benefit from developing a resource team.

 Tips from the Toolbox

Discuss with your daughter the importance of a resource team. The following activity is one way to help her develop her team.

Have your daughter assess her strengths and note where she needs help. Then, list people that could make a dramatic difference in her future. Ask her to write at least one reason why she wants them on her team, highlighting their strengths. She can include certain friends, teachers, coaches, clergy, or even you. Both diverse and similar players have their place on her team. A diverse list of players will give her a broad range of contacts and experiences from which to draw and those with similar talents and experiences will give her a deeper concentration of expertise.

Building Confidence

----

*"You have to have confidence in your ability, and then
be tough enough to follow through."* — Rosalynn Carter

Walt Disney was fired by a newspaper for not being creative enough.
Albert Einstein failed an examination that would have allowed him to study for
a diploma as an electrical engineer in Zurich. Winston Churchill failed the
sixth grade. Thomas Edison was told that he was too stupid to learn anything.
Beethoven's teacher told him that he would be hopeless as a composer. What
do all of these people have in common? They had persistence to forge ahead
and a belief that they could accomplish their goals despite the obstacles. If
they had not had the confidence to proceed, where would society be?
Confidence and persistence allowed these men and countless others to expand
their limits and pursue their goals.

Elihu Root once noted, "Men do not fail; they give up trying." Root, as
Theodore Roosevelt's secretary of state, realized the value of persistence
through his efforts for international peace. He understood that for many the
only difference between success and failure is persistence. His confidence and
belief in his purpose sustained his determination to persevere despite the odds
and ultimately won for him the Nobel Peace Prize in 1912.

Pursuing a goal despite difficulties or obstacles requires confidence that
the insurmountable can be achieved. This confidence develops from the "I
can" attitude. Alexander Lockhart, in his book *The Portable Pep Talk*, defines
confidence as a "growing spirit of assuredness flowing from the awareness that
you are on the right road to achievement. Confidence is a direct result of
positive experience. The more positive experiences you gain, the more confidence you will possess." Confidence is paramount to success.

Your daughter should celebrate small successes each day and use them to
reinforce her self-confidence. She may not look at the small things she

accomplishes as extraordinary. However, by appreciating minor successes, she will begin to feel good about herself and what she can achieve.

Many people fail because they lack self-confidence. Others who do not have a lot of talent become successful because they are confident. Your daughter has to believe in herself to keep on trying. Being confident that she can try and fail and still try again allows her to gain the experience necessary to achieve success. Her confidence increases as she learns from her experience. And if learning and growing is your daughter's goal, she can never fail.

If your daughter keeps doing exactly the same thing but expects different results, she will be disappointed. Successful people know that they cannot achieve a different outcome if they continue doing what they have always done. By varying the formula just enough to generate a new outcome and trying again, they increase their chances for success. Thomas Edison, when approached by a newspaper reporter with the question, "How does it feel to have failed five thousand times before discovering a long-lasting filament bulb?" looked astonished and replied, "Fail five thousand times? I did not fail five thousand times. I successfully discovered five thousand ways that it did not work." Edison's attitude of persistence, fueled by optimism and toned with a little humor, characterizes the nature of the toolbox-equipped woman.

Equipped with her Connected Inner Guide and her power tools, your daughter has what it takes to become the toolbox-equipped woman. By using her toolbox, she strengthens her confidence in many ways. She gains clarity in her decision making when she relies on the wisdom of her Connected Inner Guide. She practices her mirror talk to become the woman she envisions. When she knows her goals and purposes as set forth in her Lifetime Strategic Plan, she confidently pursues her objectives. These are just a few of the many ways your daughter can use her tools to become the toolbox-equipped woman. More and more, as she follows her Connected Inner Guide and maximizes the use of her power tools, you will notice a marked increase in your daughter's self-confidence.

SELF-WORTH AND CONFIDENCE

Psychologist and author Tom G. Stevens, Ph.D., sums up self-worth and the added bonus of confidence with these words, from his book *You Can Choose to Be Happy.*

Unconditional self-worth is not dependent upon who we are,
what we do, what we have, or what anyone thinks about us.
If we have self-worth, then self-confidence is a bonus.
Self-confidence is based upon our belief that we have
the right motivation, knowledge, and skills to reach our goals.
The best kind of self-confidence is knowing that
we have the *basic motivation and ability to learn* in any situation.
What began as empathy and unconditional self-love
forms the basis for self-confidence in all areas of life.
That self-caring and self-confidence provides the power of a mighty
river for overcoming life's logjams.

Building Integrity

"Keep true, never be ashamed of doing right;
decide on what you think is right and stick to it." — George Eliot

People in today's society espouse values like truth and integrity, but often when faced with deceit and wrongdoing, they turn their heads in silence. When given the opportunity to stand up for what is right, many people acquiesce into a complacent "live and let live" ambiguity. In this culture, poor character prevails and honor is an endangered commodity. But this does not have to be the case.

There is an old-fashioned remedy for poor character — build honor. It is a process that anyone can benefit from. Note the word *process*. Nobody is born with honor. Nobody gains it overnight. Building honor is a lifetime journey to develop integrity by acting in worthy ways. In the past, people who viewed themselves as having integrity and honor felt good about themselves. As honorable people, they conducted themselves in ways worthy of respect. People of honor recognized other people of honor as worthy. Character was built with each honorable action.

With your daughter's every action comes the opportunity to act with integrity. In each situation, there is a defining moment of choice — an instant where a decision must be made whether to act based on the critical, crybaby, creepy components of the unhealthy Connected Inner Guide, or to act from a place of honor. She gains strength and confidence in her decision making when she relies on her honor to guide her in this moment of choice.

Honor can be defined in terms of one's volition and actions. Honor is unquestionable integrity, truthfulness, trustworthiness, personal responsibility, dependability, and soundness of moral principle. According to Blaine Lee, author of *The Power Principle*, "We live with honor when we are true to what we believe is right.... We are on our honor when we accept and acknowledge personal responsibility for our actions. When we are honorable, we are worthy of being honored. We are honest, upright, and sincere. We are faithful to our cause, purpose, or belief."

Sometimes, acting honorably is difficult for a teen who wants to be accepted, needed, and included. Pressure to be part of the group can interfere with acting with integrity. When belonging to the group is at the expense of the right thing to do, belonging compromises the wisdom of the Connected Inner Guide and weakens honor. Acting honorably is not always easy or without price.

Being nice to keep the peace should not compromise character. While being nice is desirable in most circumstances, it never requires your daughter to be a pushover. A nice person is someone who is considerate of others, yet assertive about her principles and values. Nice should not be the ultimate goal in decision making. If your daughter has to choose between being nice and having honor, honor should always win.

Traditionally, young women have been socialized to be people pleasers. When a young woman derives her sole identity from pleasing others and uses this as a measuring tool for her self-worth, she may incur extensive damage. Putting others' needs and opinions first at the expense of personal values can harm character and lower self-worth. The feeling of only being worthy when pleasing others is counterfeit esteem. This external sense of worth thrives with praise and plummets with criticism. Relying on others' fickle approval can place a young woman's self-worth on an emotional roller coaster that is easily derailed. By drawing strength and self-worth from personal honor, your daughter can choose not to ride this roller coaster.

There is a difference between reputation and character. Character is found within. Reputation is grounded in the opinions of others. Teacher, theologian, and author Edwin A. Abbott distinguishes between character and reputation when he notes, "Character is injured by temptations, and by wrongdoing; reputation by slanders, and libels. Character endures throughout defamation in every form, but perishes when there is a voluntary transgression; reputation may last through numerous transgressions, but be destroyed by a single, and even an unfounded, accusation or aspersion."

Others can malign your daughter's reputation with founded or unfounded accusations. However, when your daughter acts with integrity, her character remains unscathed. Your daughter's character can only be damaged from her own actions.

Tremendous power comes from being an honorable person, from the simplicity of knowing the right thing to do. Honor is like giving your daughter's Trained Conscience a pair of glasses. Honor eliminates some choices (mostly poor ones) and magnifies other choices (the intrinsic right thing to do). Decision making becomes unobstructed by the clarity that honor provides.

When your daughter's Connected Inner Guide is fortified with honor, two of the Connected Inner Guide's three components immediately recognize its value and are strengthened by integrity. Her Trained Conscience, composed of her adopted universal principles and personal values, esteems honor and uses its clarity to defeat the Creep. The head's Comforter embraces honor and confronts the Critic with the intrinsic right thing to do. This makes the Toxic Inner Critic unable to rationalize and justify poor choices.

However, the heart component of the Connected Inner Guide may initially create a problem. Your daughter may find her Crybaby Heart afraid to stand up for what is right, angry that she has to be the one to do it. Her Crybaby Heart could feel misplaced guilt that she might hurt someone in the process. Now is the time for her to calm the Crybaby Heart with the reasoning of the Comforter and the moral strength of the Trained Conscience for honor to prevail.

Developing honor is a process that takes place incrementally. Building a wall of honor will help your daughter build strength, confidence, and integrity. Some of the bricks that your daughter can use to build her wall of honor are listed at right.

Each of these bricks helps strengthen your daughter's wall of honor. As the builder of her wall, she may choose which type of brick she needs and how many. The more bricks she uses, the stronger her wall. With each brick, she builds the strength, confidence, and integrity to become a toolbox-equipped woman.

BRICKS IN THE WALL OF HONOR

The goodness of decency
The courage of convictions
The strength of purpose
The power of self-control
The message of honesty
The pride of hard work
The protection of character
The energy of health
The heartiness of humor
The prudence of caution
The discipline of struggle
The wisdom of moderation
The effectiveness of simplicity
The resilience of enthusiasm
The advantage of planning
The satisfaction of generosity
The electric current of optimism
The support of friendship
The illumination of wisdom
The spirit of kindness
The productivity of teamwork
The rest of spirituality
The benefit of ambition
The merit of patience
The gratification of serving
The control of confidence
The reward of perseverance
The delight of winning
The sportsmanship of losing
The impact of choice
The liberation of forgiveness
The activity of gratitude
The treasure of unconditional love
The solidity of faith

The Toolbox-Equipped Woman

"I have found that great people do have in common . . . an immense belief
in themselves and in their mission. They also have great determination as well as
an ability to work hard. At the crucial moment of decision, they draw on their
accumulated wisdom. Above all, they have integrity." — Yousuf Karsh

You may be wondering what toolbox-equipped women look like, or even if
they exist. The good news is they are alive and well. You can spot them almost
anywhere. They may be rich or poor, a next-door neighbor or a woman living
halfway around the world. They may be from any racial, ethnic, or religious
group. They can have any career and do anything. They are your sisters, your
mothers, your cousins, your friends. While they may look like everybody else,
they have distinct qualities and characteristics. They comprise a diverse group
yet are connected by a common thread. All share wisdom — they are equipped
with a toolbox. How can you recognize toolbox-equipped women? When you
get to know these special women, this is what you will find.

They have strength. They enjoy working hard to accomplish goals. Because
they see the big picture, they don't get caught up in day-to-day business at the
expense of their vision and mission. They have a plan based on their
principles and aspirations, and implement it methodically. When there is a
tough job to do, these are the women you can count on. You can depend on
toolbox-equipped women because they are trustworthy and strong in hard
moments. Their "I can" attitude gets the job done and motivates others. They
are an inspiration. People watch and try to emulate them. Their attitude is con-
tagious. Toolbox women are grateful for what they have and express few
regrets. They enjoy humor, use it constructively, and know how to laugh at
themselves. They diligently work at being active and stress free. Part of their
daily routine involves maintaining good health, getting enough sleep, and
eating well. Their strength radiates from within.

They have confidence. Toolbox-equipped women are comfortable in a group or by themselves. They love life, every aspect of it, and live in the present. They are free from envy and truly like who they are. Their decisions are not based on anger, fear, or guilt. They make balanced, integrated decisions using positive thoughts, emotions, and values. Toolbox-equipped women's decisions are reasonable and compassionate, and their decisions benefit others as well. While these women carefully evaluate risks, they are not afraid to forge new paths. When toolbox-equipped women make mistakes, they view them as opportunities to learn and improve. They forgive others and themselves because they know that forgiveness is a gift they give themselves. Because toolbox-equipped women are not threatened by criticism, they can realistically evaluate others' suggestions. They do not need or seek others' approval. They are comfortable with their independence because they have earned it.

They have integrity. Toolbox-equipped women are credible and highly principled. They assume personal responsibility for their thoughts and actions and avoid blaming and complaining. They respect life in all its forms and consistently practice the Golden Rule. Resting in their spirituality gives them peace and companionship. People can trust them to keep their word and stand up for what they think is right. Toolbox-equipped women are loyal in their relationships and treat everyone with respect. They exhibit good sportsmanship in victory as well as defeat. Success to them is measured internally, not by possessions. Honor is the word that comes to mind when describing toolbox-equipped women.

Toolbox-equipped women exhibit strength, confidence, and integrity with every action and every word. They rely on their power tools and Connected Inner Guides to direct them in all of their endeavors. Their power tools provide an intensified richness to life that enhances an already sound foundation. These lifetime skills permeate their characters and are evidenced as the driving force behind their actions.

Toolbox-equipped women are intimately in touch with their Connected Inner Guides. They know every aspect about these guides — there are no surprises. Their Connected Inner Guides are such indispensable friends and companions that relying on them is second nature. Having decision-making skills in place is essential not only to make the best possible decisions, but also to free up time and energy to actualize, realize, and maximize higher meaning and fulfillment in life. The knowledge and wisdom that toolbox-equipped women gain from their Connected Inner Guides set them apart from others and are their defining characteristics.

The archetype of a woman equipped with a toolbox may seem to be unattainable perfection. But with practice and your support, this is a realistic and reachable possibility for your daughter. She *can* become a toolbox-equipped woman. But like any goal, first she has to choose to become one.

Perhaps, one of the best gifts you can give your daughter is the ability to choose wisely. The peace that comes from knowing that she is making sound decisions is one of the greatest blessings you can receive. And someday your blessing may be multiplied further as you see her cultivate these capabilities in your granddaughter.

The greatest gift that we could wish for you is the ability to teach your daughter how to make strong, confident decisions fueled with integrity. This book is about that journey, and we encourage you as you are well on your way.

THINK — BELIEVE — DREAM — DARE

Quoted from Walt Disney.

Think. Research, explore, question, contemplate.

Believe. Believe in yourself with undaunted faith that you can.

Dream. Dreams are the forerunners of reality. Dream big and expect positive results.

Dare. Have the courage to do. Try. Then try again. Dream your dreams believing all the while that they will come true. Base them on the same values and principles on which you base your life.

Permission Acknowledgments

Medieval Jewish poem excerpted from "God's Voice" by Scott Anstadt, Ph.D. Inner Self Magazine. Internet: www.innerself.com/Spirituality/gods _voice.html.

"The Golden Eagle." Excerpted from *The Song of the Bird* by Anthony de Mello. New York: Doubleday Publishing, 1984. Reprinted with permission of Doubleday.

Fosdick, Harry Emerson. "Six Points to Determine Right from Wrong." Paraphrased from an excerpt of a sermon preached by Dr. Fosdick at The Riverside Church, October 30, 1932. Copyright ©1932. Reprinted with permission from Dr. Elinor Fosdick Downs.

Maas, James B., Ph.D. "Are you getting enough sleep?" paraphrased from *Power Sleep*. New York: HarperCollins Publishers, Inc., 1999. Reprinted with permission of Dr. James B. Maas.

McKay, Matthew and Fanning Patrick. *Self Esteem*. Oakland, Calif.: New Harbinger Publications. Copyright © 1987. (800) 748-6273. Reprinted with permission from New Harbinger Publications, Oakland, CA.

Riera, Michael. *Uncommon Sense for Parents with Teenagers*. Berkeley, Calif.: Celestial Arts. Copyright © 1995. Reprinted with permission from Ten Speed Press, Berkeley, CA.

Scott, Sharon. "Three Steps to Overcoming Peer Pressure." Excerpted from *Peer Pressure Reversal* by Sharon Scott. Amherst, Mass.: HRD Press, Inc. Copyright © 1997. (800) 822-2801. Reprinted with permission from Sharon Scott.

Shoffstall, Veronica. "After a While." Copyright © 1971. Reprinted with permission from Veronica Shoffstall.

Staniforth, Jeffrey. "Guide to Affirmations." Internet: http://www.newage. com.au/library/affirm.html. Reprinted with permission from Jeffrey Staniforth.

Stevens, Tom G. "Self Esteem and Confidence." Excerpted from *You Can Choose to Be Happy*. By Tom G. Stevens, Ph.D. Seal Beach, Calif.: Wheeler Sutton Publishing, Copyright © 1998. Reprinted with permission from Dr. Tom G. Stevens.

Summary of "The Spiritual Dozen." Adapted from *Real Magic: Creating Miracles in Everyday Life* by Dr. Wayne W. Dyer. Copyright © 1992 by Wayne W. Dyer. Reprinted by permission of HarperCollins Publishers, Inc.

"Twelve Foods You Should Eat Before a Test." Excerpted from *The Book of Lists for Kids* by Sandra and Harry Choron. Boston: Houghton Mifflin Co., Copyright © 1995. Reprinted with permission from Houghton Mifflin Co. All rights reserved.

"What Is Your Sleep I.Q.?" Published by the National Sleep Foundation. Reprinted with permission from the National Sleep Foundation, Washington, D. C. Copyright © 1998.

Bibliography

Allen, Richard, M.D., as quoted in "Teens Hit Books, Not Pillows," by Mary Carskadon. *The Houston Chronicle*, 5 May 1995, 8 (advertising supplement).

Ash, Mary Kay. *Mary Kay on People Management.* New York: Warner, 1985.

Baum, L. Frank, and William Wallace Denslow, illus., *The Wonderful Wizard of Oz.* Chicago: George M. Hill Company, 1900.

Benson, Herbert. *The Relaxation Response.* New York: Hearst Corporation, 1976.

Brown, Lyn Mikel, and Carol Gilligan. *Meeting at the Crossroads: Women's Psychology and Girls Development.* New York: Random House, Inc., 1993.

Burns, David D., M.D. *Feeling Good.* New York: William Morrow & Co., 1999.

Buscaglia, Leo. *Loving Each Other: The Challenge of Human Relationships.* New York: Random House, 1986.

Carroll, Lewis and John Tenniiel, illus., *Alice's Adventure in Wonderland.* London: The Clarendon Press for Macmillan, 1865.

Carskadon, Mary. "Teens Hit Books Not Pillows," *The Houston Chronicle*, 5 May 1995, 8 (advertising supplement).

Chadwell, David. "Gratitude Blesses the Grateful." Internet: http://www.west-arkchurchofchrist.org/chadwell/1996/120196am.htm.

Cohen-Sandler, Roni, and Michelle Silver. *I'm Not Mad, I Just Hate You! A New Understanding of Mother-Daughter Conflict.* New York: Viking, 1999.

Chodron, Pema. "In the Gap between Right and Wrong." Internet, http://www.sinc.sunysb.edu/Clubs/buddhism/daily_main.html.

Choron, Sandra, and Harry Charon. *The Book of Lists for Kids.* Boston: Houghton Mifflin Company, 1995.

Cooper, Cynthia. Lecture. Through the Looking Glass series. The Junior League of North Harris County, Inc., 1997.

Covey, Sean. *The Seven Habits of Highly Effective Teens: The Ultimate Teenage Success Guide.* New York: Simon and Schuster, Inc., 2000.

Covey, Stephen R. *First Things First.* New York: Simon and Schuster, Inc., 1995.

Covey, Stephen R., and Sandra Merill Covey. *The Seven Habits of Highly Effective Families: Building a Beautiful Family Culture in a Turbulent World.* New York: Golden Books Publishing Company, Inc., 1997.

Craven, Margaret. *I Heard the Owl Call My Name.* New York: Dell Publishing, Inc., 1974.

De Mello, Anthony. *The Song of the Bird.* New York: Doubleday Publishing, 1984.

Dillon, Dennis. "Gratitude at the Soup Line." Internet: http://www.bible-infonet.org/ff/articles/living/111_03_23.html.

Dumont, Larry, M.D. "Groups, Gangs, and Teenage Growing Pains." *Healing Magazine,* Fall/Winter 1997, 2.

Dyer, Wayne. *Your Erroneous Zones.* New York: HarperCollins Publishers, Inc., 1993.

————. *Real Magic: Creating Miracles in Everyday Life.* New York: Harper Collins Publishers, Inc., 1993.

Eberlein, Tamara. "Think Positive: How to Be an Optimist." *Good Housekeeping.* January 1996, 77–80.

Franklin, Benjamin. "The Morals of Chess," 1779. Internet: http://www.orgs.bucknell.edu/chessclub/morals

Gayle, Lisa. "Eating Disorders and Our Children." Internet: http://family.go.com/Features/family_1997_03/metp/metp199703_eating /metp199703_eating.html.

Goulston, Mark, and Philip Goldberg. "Beat Self Defeat." *Ladies Home Journal.* March 1996, 60–62.

Graham, Jennifer. "Tired of Being Tired." *Woman's Day.* 1 September 1994, 42–44.

Halberstam, Joshua. *Everyday Ethics: Inspired Solutions to Real-Life Dilemmas.* New York: Penguin, 1994.

Handly, Jane, Robert Handly, and Pauline Neff. *Why Women Worry and How to Stop.* New York: Prentice-Hall, Inc., 1990.

"Here's a Few Things You Should Know about Playing Sports." Girl Tech. Internet: http://www.girltech.com/Sports/SP_menu_frame.html.

Jeffers, Susan. *Feel the Fear and Do It Anyway.* New York: Fawcett Columbine Book Group, 1987.

Kaplan, Leslie S. *Coping with Peer Pressure.* Center City, Minn.: Hazelden Information & Educational Services, 1997.

Kaufman, Barry Neil. *Happiness Is a Choice.* New York: Random House, Inc., 1993.

Kollar, Linda. "Violent Acts Should Never Be Excused." American Medical Association "Teen Talk." Internet: http://www.ama-assn.org/insight/h_focus/adl_hlth/teen/13teen4.htm.

Kopelman, Orion Mosha. *The Second Ten Commandments: Your Guide to Success in the Consciousness Age.* Palo Alto, Calif.: Global Brain, Inc., 1999.

Lee, Blaine. *The Power Principle: Influence with Honor.* New York: Simon and Schuster, Inc., 1997.

"Less Stress Handbook." Tylenol pamphlet, 1992.

Lewis, Michael, as quoted in "Why You Are Feeling Stressed," by Carla Rohlfing. *Family Circle,* 22 September 1992, 81–82.

Lockhart, Alexander. *The Portable Pep Talk.* Richmond, Va.: Zander Press, 1997.

Maas, James. *Power Sleep.* New York: HarperCollins Publishers, Inc., 1999.

McGraw, Phillip. *Life Strategies: Doing What Works, Doing What Matters.* New York: Hyperion Press, 2000.

McIlhaney, Joe S., Jr., and Debra W. Haffner. "Are Abstinence-Only Sex-Education Programs Good for Teenagers? Yes!" *Insight on the News.* 13, no. 36 (September 29, 1997): 24. Internet: http://www.abcog.org/abstain.htm.

McKay, Matthew, and Patrick Fanning. *Self-Esteem.* Oakland, Calif.: New Harbinger Publications, 1987.

More, Max. "Dynamic Optimism." Extropy Institute, 1997. Internet: http://www.extropy.com/do.htm. Revised from original "Dynamic Optimism" in Extropy 8, 1990.

———. "Dynamic Optimism: Philosophy and Psychology for Shattering Limits." 24 July 1999. Internet: http://www.awarenessmag.com/so_dynam.htm.

Mosbacher, Georgette, as quoted in *Miracle of Change: The Path to Self-Discovery and Spiritual Growth,* by Dennis Wholey. New York: Simon and Schuster, Inc., 1998.

"Muhammed Ali. 'The Greatest.'" Sports Placement Services, Inc. Internet: http://www.sportsplacement.com/ali.htm.

Murphy, Ann Pleshette. "Ten Parenting Resolutions." *Good Morning America.* 3 January 2000.

Newman, Winifred. Internet: http://graceland.gentle.org/quotes2.html

"Omnibus Sleep in America Poll, 1998." The National Sleep Foundation. Internet:http://www.sleepfoundation.org/publications/1998poll.html.

Owens, Karen. "Six Myths about Self-Esteem." *Journal of Invitational Theory and Practice,* 4, no. 2 (1997): 115. Abridged by Bob Reasoner.

Parachin, V. M. "Ten Steps to Self-Esteem." *Your Health.* 33, No. 24, 76–79.

———. "Talking Turkey about Thanksgiving: We Need a Gratitude Attitude Adjustment." *The Lutheran.* Internet: http://www.thelutheran.org/9711/page26.html.

Peale, Norman Vincent, as quoted in "The Eternal Optimist," by Jeanne Pugh. *St. Petersburg Times.* Religion Section, 8 June 1985.

Peter, Laurence J., and Bill Dana. *The Laughter Prescription: How to Achieve Health, Happiness, and Peace of Mind through Humor.* New York: Ballantine Publishing Group, 1982.

Peterson, Karen S. "Plumbing the Depths of Depression among Teens." *USA Today,* 9 April 1996. Internet: http://www.usatoday.com/life/health/lhs450.htm.

Pipher, Mary. *Reviving Ophelia.* New York: Ballantine Publishing Group, 1994.

Pitts, Leonard, Jr. "What's Happening to Girls Makes You Want to Weep." *Houston Chronicle,* 28 July 1997, A21.

Plecha, Brenola, as quoted in "Eating Disorders and Our Children," by Lisa

Gayle. Internet: http://family.go.com/Features/family_1997_03/
metp/metp199703_eating/metp199703_eating.html.

Rand, Ayn. *Atlas Shrugged.* New York: The Penguin Group, 1992.

Reasoner, Robert. "Review of Self-Esteem Research." National Association of
Self-Esteem. Internet: http://www.self-esteem-nase.org/research.html.

Reiman, Joey. *Success: The Original Handbook.* Marietta, Ga.: Longstreet
Press, Inc., 1992.

Rhoades, George F. "Controlling the Volcano Within." *The Anger Management
Newsletter.* Internet: http://www.anger-management.net.

Riera, Michael. *Uncommon Sense for Parents with Teenagers.* Berkeley, Calif.:
Celestial Arts, 1995.

Roger, John, and Peter McWilliams. *Focus on the Positive.* Los Angeles,
Calif.: Prelude Press, 1992.

Rohlfing, Carla. "The Healing Power of Being Nice." *Family Circle.*
1 September 1995, 26–27.

———. "Why You're Feeling Stressed." *Family Circle,* 22 September 1992,
81–82.

"Role Models on the Web: Sadako Ogata. Internet: http://www.news/tr.com/
rolemodel/ogata/sogata.html.

"Role Models on the Web: Diane Sawyer. Internet: http://www.news/tr.com/
rolemodel/sawyer/dsawyer.html.

Rosch, Paul, M.D. American Institute of Stress. Internet: http://www.stress.org.

Rubin, T. I., as quoted in *Miracle of Change,* by Dennis Wholey. New York:
Simon and Schuster, Inc., 1998.

Scott, Sharon. "Three Steps to Overcome Peer Pressure." Excerpted from *Peer
Pressure Reversal* by Sharon Scott. Amhurst, Mass.: HRD Press, Inc.,
1997. (800) 822-2801

"Self-Image: The Fantasy, The Reality." Discussion Guide. *In the Mix.* Public
Broadcasting System special. Internet: http://www.pbs.org/inthemix
/educators/fant_real.html.

Seligman, Martin. E. P. *Learned Optimism.* New York: Simon and Schuster,
Inc., 1998.

"Seligman: Optimism Can Be a Vaccination," *APA Monitor* (American
Psychology Association). Internet: http://www.apa.org/monitor/
oct96/marty.html

"Shortchanging Girls, Shortchanging America." American Association of University Women report. 1991.

Smith, Susan Male. "Food: The New Stress Therapy." *Family Circle*, 22 September 1992, 88.

Stamb, Erwin, and James Wasco. "The Lowdown of Anxiety." *Woman's Day*, 11 August 1992, 15.

Shoffstall, Veronica. "After a While." Copyright © 1971.

Staniforth, Jeffrey. "Guide to Affirmations." Internet: http://www.newage.com. au/library/affirm.html.

"Statistical Abstract of the United States, Dept. of Commerce Bureau of the Census, 1997." Tab. 317.

Stevens, Tom G. *You Can Choose to Be Happy*. Seal Beach, Calif.: Wheeler Sutton Publishing, 1998.

Stewart, Page, and Katherine Lafreniere, as quoted in "Roots of Optimism," by Anne Bilodeau. *Self-Help and Psychology Magazine*. Internet: http://www.shpm.com/articles/depress/deopti.html.

Taylor, Amy. "Becoming Fulfilled." *Inner Self Magazine*. Internet: http://www.innerself.com/spirituality/becoming_fulfilled.html.

"Trends in Teen Nutrition." IFIC. Internet: http://ificinfo.health.org/insight /teentrnd.htm.

"Unwind Before You Unravel." *Houston Chronicle*, Lifestyle. 23 August 1992, 6.

Ward, William Arthur. "To Do Nothing." Internet: http://www.joyfulliving services.com/todonothing.html.

Wechsler, Harlan J. *What's So Bad about Guilt?* New York: Simon and Schuster, Inc., 1990.

"What Is Your Sleep IQ?" The National Sleep Foundation Archives. Washington, D.C., July 23, 1997.

White, Gregory L., and Paul E. Mullen. *Jealousy: Theory, Research, and Clinical Strategies*. New York: Guilford Publications, Inc., 1998.

Wholey, Dennis. *Miracle of Change*. New York: Simon and Schuster, Inc., 1998.

Wooten, Patty. "Humor: An Antidote for Stress." *Holistic Nursing Practice*, 10, no. 2, 49–55. Reprinted on the Internet: Jest for the Health of It. http://www.jesthealth.com/artantistress.html.

Ziglar, Zig. *Raising Positive Kids in a Negative World*. New York: Ballantine Books, 1989.

Index

D

E

F

 nnette Geffert and Diane Brown have dedicated over twenty years to enriching the lives of women and children. Their volunteer efforts brought them together twelve years ago in the pursuit of developing children's confidence and character. Through their shared efforts, they became aware of the enormous challenges facing teens today and the associated decline of girls' self-esteem as they approach adolescence. Their shared vision in rectifying this debilitating problem led them on an extensive research project that culminated in this book. As mothers of three daughters, ages thirteen through twenty-one, and two adolescent sons, the writing of this book was a heartfelt calling. Both Diane and Annette continue to focus their energies on women's issues, in particular developing leadership skills in women. Diane received a master's degree in public administration from the University of Georgia, and Annette received a business administration degree from the University of Houston. Annette and Diane currently reside with their families in Houston, Texas.